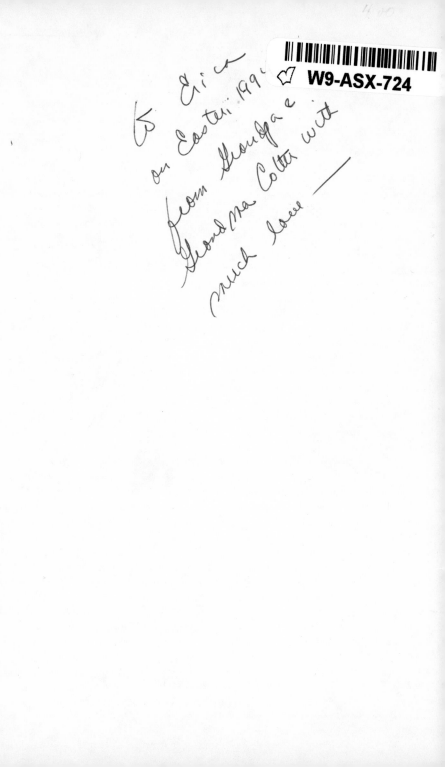

To Erica
on Easter 1990
from Grandpa &
Grandma Cotter with
much love

HEROES FROM EVERY WALK OF LIFE

HEROES
FROM
EVERY
WALK
OF
LIFE

profiles of great men and women

by the Daughters of St. Paul

ST. PAUL EDITIONS

NIHIL OBSTAT:
   Rev. Richard V. Lawlor, S.J.
   Censor Deputatus

IMPRIMATUR:
   + Humberto Cardinal Medeiros
   Archbishop of Boston

Library of Congress Cataloging in Publication Data
Main entry under title:

Heroes from every walk of life.

   1. Catholics—Biography.   I. Daughters of St.
Paul.
BX4651.2.H47   282'.092'2   [B]   81-2125   AACR2
ISBN 0-8198-3303-7 cloth
      0-8198-3304-5 paper

Printed in U.S.A. by the Daughters of St. Paul
50 St. Paul's Ave., Boston, MA 02130

The Daughters of St. Paul are an international congregation of religious
women serving the Church with the communications media.

CONTENTS

the
woman
aflame—
St. Madeleine
Sophie
Barat

"Wow! Look at that!" Leaving a conspicuous nose-print on the attic window, eleven-year-old Louis Barat whirled around toward Marie-Louise. Her face reflected the eerie, red glow that lit up the sky.

"It's awful, Louis! I'm scared!"

A *fire!* This was the most exciting thing that might ever happen in his whole lifetime, thought Louis desperately, and his sister wouldn't even *enjoy* it!

"Oh, do you have to be such a...a...girl!" he moaned.

Only feet away, a fiery plank crashed to the ground, where crackling tongues of flame devoured it.

"It might get to our house, Louis!" worried Marie-Louise.

"Naw, it's almost out. Pierre said it's under control," Louis continued with a tone of disappointment. "Maybe *now* I can carry some water buckets...." And in a flash he was down the stairs and bolting across the kitchen.

"You're staying right in this house, young man." It was his father.

Louis swallowed his explanation. There was no use asking again. Jacques Barat ruled with a father's authority, yet he wasn't unreasonable.

"I might need you, son," confided Mr. Barat. "Your new brother or sister will be here soon—very soon."

Temporarily the fire was forgotten. Louis began to think of all the help he could be.... And his father was right. In no time at all a new baby sister was lustily announcing her appearance. Just like the fire, she had been unexpected.

"She's two months early. That's why she's so terribly small, and frail..." Jacques Barat reassured himself. "It's understandable." Still, there was no point in taking chances.

"Louis, run to church and ask Father if he'll baptize the baby first thing tomorrow morning...."

Louis didn't have to be told twice. He was already half-way out the door when Mr. Barat's strong voice sounded again, "...and—no detours!"

The priest looked at the small boy panting before him.

"I'll be ready and glad to do it, son. But what about godparents?"

The godmother was already chosen. But the godfather... With more than half the town still smoldering, and the fire not out yet, it wouldn't be easy to find a man available.

"*Me*, Father! I'll be her godfather," Louis volunteered between breaths. "I'm going to be a priest, Father. I'll take *real* good care of her, I promise!"

The priest hesitated, then agreed.

Louis ran home as fast as he could. "I get to be her godfather!" he chanted over and over. Why, this was more exciting than a fire any day!

Madeleine Sophie Barat often heard the grown-ups reminiscing about the events of her birth. Soon it became the family tradition to have visiting relatives and friends ask the little girl, "And what brought you into the world, Sophie?" They loved her invariable answer, "It was fire." Little then did Sophie Barat realize just how right she was. Fire had started her life, and fire was to characterize the whole of it.

Louis kept his promise and went off to the seminary. He also kept his promise of taking very good care of his sister-godchild, which at times Sophie may almost have regretted. The zealous seminarian had definite ideas about his sister's education, and when he studied Latin, Greek, Hebrew and a host of other subjects, so did she. He wasn't her godparent for nothing, and if her name— Sophie—meant "wisdom," he'd do all in his power to see that she got it!

The French Revolution, narrow escapes from death, prison, ordination. Through it all, Louis Barat did not forget his little sister. When he returned home, a priest at last, his little sister wasn't little any longer. She was an attractive and willful teenager.

One evening, soon after his arrival, Louis sat down to talk with his parents. Sophie, he explained, seemed to have an aptitude for studies. Could she, did they think, go to Paris with him? There, under Mademoiselle Duval, she could continue her studies and he, Louis, could direct her and prepare her for her future.

Paris—in Sophie's estimation—meant the hotbed of the Revolution. Blood ran in the streets. The infamous guillotine wasn't so long out of service that it couldn't be used again. Morals were at an all-time low. It was so obvious, Sophie told herself and her brother, that everything was in favor of her *not* going. She was religious, and the public practice of religion was still forbidden in the capital. She had always lived in the country; she just *knew* she wouldn't like the stuffy, old city. Besides, how could she leave her mother and father? She was only sixteen!

But if Sophie had a will of iron, her brother's was stronger still. Louis went to Paris. And Sophie went with him.

It wasn't all that bad in Paris. Mademoiselle Duval, with whom Sophie took up residence, was a wonderful woman. At a time when even wearing a cross could have cost her her head, she had turned part of her home into a chapel. She had courage and stamina, and Sophie loved those qualities.

The chapel was wonderful. And there was also a workshop for poor girls. Sophie began to help teach them reading, writing, sewing and, of course, religion. That was her favorite class. There was a steady rhythm of study, work, teaching and praying.

And Paris wasn't the terrible, ungodly place she had imagined it to be, but it was secular. If her upstairs room kept her out of earshot of the revolutionary propaganda and irreligious vulgarities of the streets, it didn't keep her from noticing the ladies' fashions. A pretty, grecian-style dress caught her eye one day. It was *so* feminine, so much more graceful than the coarse, country skirts she had always known....

Sophie was unusually intent on her work. And Marguerite was dying of curiosity. She found an excuse to go to the window-cabinet and get a good look at what Sophie was sewing. Why, it was just one of the little girls' frocks. How dull!

"Where's the lovely dress you were working on the other day?" Marguerite asked.

Sophie reddened.

"Oh, come on, Sophie, tell me!" coaxed her companion. "Where is it?"

Sophie said nothing, then changed the subject. But Marguerite's curiosity was going to be satisfied. Finally, eyes still on her work, Sophie said softly, "Where my stupid vanity should be—in the fire." "No!" gasped Marguerite. "But, Sophie, it was *gorgeous!* Who on earth did it?..." She stopped short. "Oh, no, don't tell me! It was that brother of yours. Am I ever glad *I* don't have a brother," she said with relief.

But Sophie indulged in no self-pity. After all, she wanted to belong to God, and Louis was just seeing to it that she did. Grecian crepe gowns weren't exactly preparation for the convent.

Oh, to be a nun, sighed Sophie. The trouble was, there weren't any nuns around. The Revolution had dispersed them all. Convents, monasteries and religious buildings of every kind were tumble-down ruins or civil property. Oh, there were still priests and religious, but they were working underground, in hiding, like her brother. Still, Sophie was sure of her vocation. And if it was a gift from God, as she knew it was, God Himself would show her the way.

Seven springs had blossomed into seven summers. Much had taken place in the life of the young country girl since her coming to Paris. The unknown, unorganized little group at Mademoiselle Duval's was, through dint of changes, maturation and normal growing pains, fast taking shape as a real religious community with well-defined goals.

The Revolution and the terror sweeping in its wake had broken bodies and minds. The horrible memories of the offenses to God and the tremendous spiritual hunger that ravaged the people—especially the children—burned themselves into Sophie's already ardent soul.

But more than zealous desires burned within Sophie. Pain did also. Pain far greater than what she had felt when Louis had flung her beautiful dress into the fire, and hopefully with it, her vanity.

The priest who directed the little nucleus of religious had one day questioned them on the catechism. He had asked Sophie the most elementary question: Why did God make you? And she had answered, "To know Him, to love Him and to serve Him...."

"What does it mean to serve God?" the priest had queried further.

Her answer was simple. "Doing God's will."

"Right." The priest's voice took on tones of authority. "And God's will is that you be Superior."

The young women were delighted. These sisters had no name, no house, no habit, but they had a superior. While they managed to restrain their joy, Sophie burst into tears.

Father was inflexible. "You will do God's will, *Mother* Barat," he told the twenty-three-year-old nun.

Fire had marked her birth. Fire characterized her temperament. Fire, too, had perhaps been the silent instrument which had turned her away from herself and the world and had catapulted her into an unquenchable furnace: the heart of Christ.

It was this fire that refined the gold of Sophie Barat's great natural qualities. Her brilliant mind and indomitable will, the warmth of her heart—all these poured themselves into the burning heart and service of the Master.

More than sixty years after that night, Mother Barat still remembered vividly the circumstances that surrounded the beginning of her Society and the purpose for which God had called it into being:

"And so I came to the primordial idea of our little Society of the Sacred Heart: to gather together young girls and establish a community which, night and day, would adore the Heart of Jesus outraged in His Eucharis-

Her brilliant mind and indomitable will, the warmth of her heart—all these poured themselves into the burning heart and service of the Master.

tic love. But, I said, when we shall be twenty-four religious able to replace each other...to keep up perpetual adoration, that will be much. Yet it's still very little to do for such a noble purpose. But if we had pupils whom we could form to the spirit of adoration and reparation, that would be different. And I saw those hundreds, those thousands of adorers as an ideal and universal ostensorium lifted up above the Church. That is it! I said to myself before a lonely tabernacle; we must vow ourselves to the education of youth; we must lay in souls the solid foundation of lively faith in the Blessed Sacrament, and with...devotion to the Sacred Heart in the Blessed Sacrament, we shall raise up a throng of adorers from all nations and to the very ends of the earth."

Set ablaze by her, the Religious of the Sacred Heart spread from city to city, nation to nation, continent to continent, aflame with the cry that issued from Christ's own heart: "I have come to cast fire upon the earth."

After eighty-five love-filled years, the great heart of Sophie Barat burned itself out. But the spirit and the mission that fed it would burn brightly into the dawn of Eternal Light. As at its beginning, so too at its end, her life had enkindled a fire.

2

"la
marchesana"

Halls with high, vaulted ceilings, warmth, music and laughter, long tables heaped with prize game and choice wines.... It was January 17, 1403, and this was the marriage feast of the Marquis Theodore II of Montferrat and Princess Margaret of Savoy-Achaia. Margaret forced herself to enjoy it, for she was determined to make the best of this new life, even though her inclinations would have led her in another direction. As she smiled up into the eyes of her husband, she hoped ardently that this political marriage would bring peace to the war-torn countryside of Northern Italy.

Margaret had found where God's will lay. If the peace and well-being of her beloved Piedmont were to be purchased through personal sacrifice—even the renunciation of her own choice of life—then, so let it be. She had been called by God to be at the service of His people. And she was determined to go all the way. She would be their servant.

The winter wind howled as it tried in vain to gain entrance, for all was shut and barred. Inside there was peace and happiness. Margaret had found her peace in God's will. Although the initial arrangement for the marriage had come as a crushing blow, she now realized how much she loved the man whom God had destined to be her husband.

Shortly after the wedding, as was the custom of sovereigns of the time, Theodore took his wife to visit the various parts of his realm. Then they went to live at the palaces of Chivasso and Trino. It was at one of these two castles that Margaret met her two stepchildren, John Giacomo, and Sophia, Theodore's children by his previous marriage to Joanna of Lorraine, who had died just one year before.

Margaret gave herself over to her new life without any reservation. Through the grace she obtained from persevering prayer, she and Theodore became not only two in one flesh, but one mind and heart in God.

Under Margaret's gentle but insistent tactics Theodore became kinder and more patient. His sudden outbursts of anger became less and less frequent. Through love and understanding Margaret taught him to be not only a sovereign, but also a father to their people.

Margaret also had a pleasant knack for what might be termed "housecleaning." The palaces and castles of the Marquisate underwent a transformation. Only persons of high moral integrity were permitted to live within their walls. Politely but firmly, all others were asked to change their lives or seek employment elsewhere. This so-called housecleaning was even leveled against her equals. In fact, she was even more demanding of them. They were to set the example.

But there was no one with whom she was more demanding than herself. Under her stately robes of silk and brocade Margaret wore a penitential hairshirt.

She continued this practice even when, as a result of the all too common feudal wars, she became Dogaressa of Genoa. In Genoa, too, she soon amazed her subjects with her lavish charity.

One day, in conversation, Theodore unwittingly made a remark to Margaret. "Think of the precedence we have now," he said, "over the Visconti, the Lords of Saluzzo, and Ferrara and many others."

"These are passing glories, Dore," she said. "I prefer the eternal."

"Margot," he chided, "you are too old in your ways. I don't understand you."

Whether he understood her or not didn't really matter. He treasured her like a precious gem and jealously guarded her as the most valuable possession in his realm.

When the plague struck Genoa, Margaret not only provided the means to relieve the victims, but gave her own services as well. She could be seen trudging about the city, dressed in poor clothes, going to care for the sick with her own hands. She sold her finest jewels in order to buy more food for the poor. Every evening she returned to her palace utterly exhausted. Then, unmindful of her own need of rest, she spent the night on her knees in prayer or else performed corporal penances. All this was for the people she ruled and loved so dearly.

In early October, 1418, Theodore and Margaret had the honor of welcoming the Holy Father, Pope Martin V, into their Marquisate.

It was one of the happiest days of Margaret's life. *Il dolce Cristo in terra* (the sweet Christ on earth)—as Margaret's contemporary, St. Catherine of Siena, had called the Pope, had been so good as to bless the soil of Piedmont with his presence.

At this time, when Theodore should have been relaxed and happy, Margaret noticed how worn and haggard he had suddenly grown. As the bright skies of early autumn turned to the slate grey of late November, there came the awful realization that her husband was not a well man. He was continually tired and listless. His walk became increasingly slower. No more did he talk of new conquests, honors or glories. *Pax*—peace—this was the word always on his lips.

His conversations with her took on a decidedly spiritual tone. Margaret felt a strong premonition that she was about to lose this man whom she had come to love so dearly.

During the last week of November, Theodore fell unaccountably ill. Nothing Margaret did could lessen the gravity of his condition. He called his son, John Giacomo, to his bedside to give him his final words, "Fear God, observe His laws. Make justice and piety the ornaments of your throne; be kind to the poor; be vigilant in your care of our state. And, above all, take care of your mother." Then, on December 2, 1418, with crucifix in hand, Theodore went back to God.

Theodore had been twice Margaret's age and it was only obedience to God's plans that had united the two in the sacred bonds of Matrimony. By dint of pain and anxiety, patience and understanding, Margaret had learned to love. From the beginning, she had placed no obstacles in the way of their married life. She had dreamed of becoming a real mother. Having children of her own would have been a joy. But God had tried her even in that. And now, after only fifteen years of married life, she had lost her Theodore.

For two years, Margaret lived with her stepson and stepdaughter at the castle of Casale Montferrat. The responsibility of the Marquisate was no longer hers. It had been passed on to John Giacomo. She felt that she was now free to do what she had wanted to do so many years before: consecrate herself "entirely to the service of God."

John Giacomo took good care of his dear step-mother. He offered to give her any palace in the realm. Margaret chose that of Alba—an ancient and historic city dating back to 93 B.C. It had gone through many years of political intrigue by the time Margaret arrived there in October, 1420.

Margaret was not alone now. She was accompanied by a number of other noble women who wished to follow her in her new way of life. Margaret was embarking on a career that was to be a remarkable turning point in her life. The palace of Alba was soon turned into a convent, where these good sisters followed a routine of prayer and work.

At first, they were not sisters in the real sense of the word. But soon after their arrival, the bishop permitted them to make the vows of poverty, chastity and obedience and dedicate themselves to taking care of the poor and the sick.

Margaret knew that this was not all that God was asking of her. Shortly before her religious profession, she had had a vision of St. Vincent Ferrer who, accompanied by St. Dominic and St. Catherine of Siena, had told her to don the Dominican habit—first as an active religious and later as a cloistered nun. At first, the time she was to enter the cloister was not entirely clear to Margaret; but she decided to act and then let God lead her in the way He saw best.

For twenty-five years Margaret of Savoy lived her life of prayer joined to active work on behalf of the poor and underprivileged. Then the hour of God struck.

Realizing that she was no longer a young woman and that she had not as yet complied with the request of Vincent Ferrer—which was her own desire as well—Margaret finally turned to the Holy Father. On June 16, 1445, the Pope issued a Bull authorizing Margaret to found the Monastery of St. Mary Magdalen in Alba. The monastery was dedicated by the bishop of Alba in the summer of 1448, and Margaret was named Superior, a position which she held until three months before her death in 1464.

During all those years, first as an active and then as a cloistered religious, Margaret sought to lead a humble, hidden life. But her love for Christ was such that He could not fail to grant her special proofs and favors of His own love for her.

Miraculous happenings were quite evident both within and without the monastery enclosure. Margaret tried to conceal them, but it was impossible—especially when the wine cask never ran out, even though the nuns knew the supply had been exhausted by Margaret's generosity with the poor.

During the first chilly days of October, 1464, when Margaret was confined to bed, the nuns began to realize that their Foundress, Mother and Superior would not be with them much longer. They often found her with her arms outstretched, praying, "Yes, Jesus, I am coming. How beautiful You are."

Her last few days were ones of unspeakable agony. She could hardly talk. The Lord permitted her to be subjected to all sorts of temptations.

Afraid of disheartening her spiritual daughters, she tried to console them. "Do not fear, my children," she gasped between spasms of pain. "The passage is difficult but the voyage is short. Soon, in heaven, I hope to be able to repay you for all that you are doing for me."

A short time later, Margaret suddenly sat up and opened her eyes in ecstatic joy. "Jesus...Jesus!" she called. She gazed at Someone who seemed to be standing directly in front of her and carried on a conversation incomprehensible to those around her. Then she closed her eyes and fell back on her pillow; she had just a little time left.

On November 22, the nuns noticed strange lights in her room. That evening, the city was covered by a heavy blanket of snow. In the early morning hours of November 23, as the nuns rose for prayer, they were immediately summoned to Margaret's room. As soon as they arrived, they began to chant the "Salve Regina"—a beautiful, ancient hymn to God's holy Mother. As they reached the words, "O clement, O loving, O sweet Virgin Mary," Margaret of Savoy's soul returned to its Maker.

At that moment the monastery bells, of their own accord, burst forth in festive peals. Filled with mixed emotions, the townspeople thronged the streets announcing, "The saint is dead!"

The body of Blessed Margaret of Savoy Achaia now lies incorrupt in the Church of St. Mary Magdalen in Alba awaiting the joy of the final resurrection. It is mute testimony to the truth that "Nothing is impossible with God."

3

"stand by me, Meg!"

It *was* true. Margaret *was* an unusual woman. But then, she had an unusual father. What other man of sixteenth-century England could boast of such well-educated daughters? Thomas More was a man who never did things by halves, and his daughter, Meg, had inherited this trait.

Margaret More could match, and even out-match, any scholar of her day—in fact, startle the king himself—with her mastery of Latin, Greek, philosophy and other subjects deemed appropriate only for men.

More could be proud of his daughter. And he was.

Margaret was the oldest of the four children born to Thomas More and his first wife, Jane, during the six short but happy years that preceded Jane's death. That death was a tremendous personal loss for Thomas, as expressed in the affectionate inscription he had engraved on his wife's tombstone: "Dear Jane lies here, the little wife of Thomas More."

But life had to go on. And More needed a mother for his four children, the oldest of whom was five. Besides being a deeply spiritual man, the young lawyer was extremely practical. Within the space of a few months, he solved his problem by marrying Alice Middleton, a widow who combined many good qualities with a short temper and sharp tongue. People talked, as they always will, but Thomas was more concerned about his children than about popular opinions. Despite what anyone might have said or thought at first, it was soon obvious that no one loved his homelife more than Thomas More.

As Margaret and the other children grew in age, the More family grew in prestige and good fortune. Thomas More's wisdom and wit, his capacity to face up to any situation, and his ability to win every case or cause he backed, changed his status from lawyer to statesman. Indeed, by 1529, he was second in the realm to only one man—Henry VIII. For Thomas had been appointed Lord Chancellor of England.

Through these years Meg More was as close to her unusual father as a daughter could be. Not only intellectual studies, but also More's own work in law and in parliament were frequent topics of conversation at the dinner table and around the hearth of the family home in Chelsea.

When in her early teens, Margaret had already translated a treatise by the celebrated scholar Erasmus. Then at sixteen, she married William Roper, a very capable, wealthy lawyer and her intellectual equal.

Meg's stepmother, Dame Alice, the efficient but rather superficial woman Sir Thomas had married after Jane's death, would have preferred to see the young woman marry into the nobility, but Meg had tastes like her father's and would have none of it.

Yes, Meg More Roper *was* an unusual woman for those days, and though always a loving wife and mother, she was ever devoted to her father.

It was Christmas, 1529. The great hall of the terrace-top mansion in Chelsea was filled to overflowing. Brightly lit and decorated, alive with music and laughter, the warmth and joy it radiated was reflected on every face.

Meg's glance met her husband's across the crowded room and they exchanged a smile. Both turned toward the end of the great hall where Sir Thomas sat surrounded by delightfully squealing grandchildren.

He looks so happy, Meg thought to herself. And yet his heart is heavy.

More always looked happy when he was with his family—even when Dame Alice pointed a cutting remark at him, or when he was weary from a hard day at court. Only Meg could read the sorrow in his heart. Only she could understand the genius and saint who cared nothing for the honors he had received, who placed his money and his home at the disposition of the poor and homeless.

Her face clouded as she remembered a day two months before. She had run to fling her arms around her father's neck on his return home from London, where he had just received the Great Seal of the Lord Chancellor. Sir Thomas had responded to her happy embrace with, "God bless you, Meg. Yet the cause of your joy will surely be my death."

"Why so serious, Margaret?" Will Roper queried, as he came up and placed his hand on his young wife's shoulder. But Will needed no answer. He knew it already. For that matter, all England knew it. Henry VIII wanted Anne Boleyn, and being already married, he was trying to have his first marriage set aside. It looked as though he would stop at nothing; to stand in his way would mean death. But Sir Thomas More had already made it clear that he would never break faith with his God to please his king.

This was the dark cloud under which the More household now lived.

In the months that followed, one thought tugged at Meg's mind: much as she was determined to support her father in his just stand, could she hold firm if that stand were to bring about his death?

Meanwhile, in London, another woman was at work. She was an angular girl with six fingers on one hand and a grim determination to be Queen of England at all costs. She had slowly worked things her way with few exceptions. One of those exceptions was Sir Thomas More. There was no telling when the last tree would be felled.

Then came the initial blow. One May morning Sir Thomas stated with a characteristic pun, "The Lord Chancellor is no More!"

That same evening, when he was alone with Meg, Sir Thomas pleaded, "When the time comes, please, Meg, stand by me. You alone, I think, have the courage."

Meg remembered these words about two years later, when she was ushered into her father's cell in the grim Tower of London. Would she have the courage he believed she had? There in that prison when she saw how weak and sick he was, she clung to him and sobbed, "Father, please relent!"

She had failed him.

Before that devastating appeal, Sir Thomas was almost powerless. Finally he rallied and whispered, "They have played the serpent with you, Mistress Eve. They have sent you to tempt old father Adam."

Meg gasped and broke down. Sir Thomas gathered his girl into his arms to kiss her tenderly. Then they knelt down to pray together. From somewhere within, Meg drew the courage she needed to stand by her father's decision.

On July 1, 1535, Sir Thomas More was condemned to death. As her father was being escorted back to the Tower to await his execution, Meg defiantly broke through the guards and threw her arms about him for the last time.

"Meg, Meg. Have patience and do not trouble yourself. It is the will of God."

Back in prison, on July 5th, the day before his death, Sir Thomas wrote his last letter. It was to his strong and faithful Meg. "I never liked your manner toward me better than when you kissed me last. Farewell, my dear child. Pray for me, and I shall pray for you and all your friends that we may meet merrily in heaven."

The next morning, as the sun sparkled on the dew-laden grass of Tower Hill, Sir Thomas More calmly met death. His final words were a testament: "I die, the king's good servant, but God's first."

It was July 9th. In the pre-dawn darkness Meg left the More mansion at Chelsea by rowboat, accompanied by her father's secretary, John Wood. Dipping their oars softly and silently, they made their way down the foggy Thames until London Bridge loomed before them.

There it was. By the light of pitch torches, which also revealed two guards slumped over in sleep, Margaret could see the head of Sir Thomas impaled on a spike.

The little boat glided into the landing and Meg climbed ashore. With a strength and courage that almost defied reason, she pulled the head from the spike and gently placed it in a bronze urn that she had brought with her. She and Wood then rowed back up the Thames to Chelsea, where the martyr's head was buried in a secret niche.

Meg *had* stood by her father. Except for one fleeting moment of weakness, she had supported him till the end.

Margaret then collected and hid all her father's papers and writings along with her own diary. Thus she preserved for posterity a heritage that, although hers by right, became ours through her gift—the legacy of one woman's stouthearted love and selfless devotion.

4

give
us
a
mother!

It was December 9, 1531. Juan Diego, a Christian Aztec, was hiking to a nearby village for Mass. Juan was one of the few Christians among his people. He hummed a tune—a quick tune—to speed his step. Soon he reached the foot of Tepeyac Hill, which he had to cross. He stopped humming and stopped walking because something strange was happening. He heard music—soft, beautiful music. It seemed to come from the top of the hill. Juan Diego mumbled to himself, "Someone holy is near. Something strange is happening."

The Indian looked around, confusion written all over his face. The music had stopped. Someone was calling his name, "Juan...Juanito!"

Juan looked up. The voice seemed to be coming from the top of the hill. He quickly climbed it and watched in awe as a lovely lady appeared. Juan's thoughts were racing, "What a beautiful lady! ...What a beautiful lady!"

The mysterious lady wore a long pink dress brocaded in gold. A blue mantle, spangled with stars, covered her head. She also wore a gold crown. The Lady spoke, "Juan, my precious one, I am the Mother of God. For years I have looked with compassion on my poor Indians; your sorrows and tears torment my soul. Go to the bishop, Juan. Tell him it is my will that a temple in my honor be built right here!"

The Indian's face glowed as he said, "Yes, yes, beautiful Lady."

When Juan arrived at the bishop's palace in Mexico City, the servants, noticing his shabby appearance, tried to dismiss him by saying that the bishop was very busy.

"But I must see the bishop," Juan Diego insisted. "I'll wait until he's free."

Hours passed. The Indian was still waiting. The servants whispered to each other, "Send that man away!"

"I've tried that several times...he won't go! He says he won't move an inch until he sees the bishop."

"But he's so...ragged-looking. Maybe he wants food or clothing."

"I've tried that, too. He doesn't want food and he doesn't want clothes. He just wants to talk to the bishop."

Juan had to wait almost all day. But...wait he did. The bishop listened to his story. He was kind and thoughtful. But he didn't believe the Indian. Slowly Juan trudged homeward, talking to himself. When he reached Tepeyac Hill, our Lady was there waiting for him. He told her his tale of disappointment.

"I don't know what to do, Mother Mary. I am so poor and ignorant. The bishop will never believe me. Please, Mother, send a more worthy messenger, someone who is smart and rich; someone who can really impress the bishop."

Mary smiled at his simplicity and responded in her gentle way, "I have many messengers from whom I could pick, but I want *you*, Juan, and no other! Go back to the bishop tomorrow and repeat your request."

The next day found Juan back at the bishop's house. The servants made him wait a long time again before they so much as informed the bishop of his presence. This time the bishop listened to Juan more carefully. He questioned and cross-questioned the stranger. He was impressed by the Indian's sincerity and gentleness. But he explained, "You see, Juan, because of my position as bishop, I need more than *your* word for what you are asking. I cannot build a shrine for your Lady unless you obtain from her a sign to show that she is really the Mother of God."

Juan returned to his Lady and made the request. She told him to return the next day at which time she would give him a sign that would cause him to be received with joy. But Juan returned home to find his uncle gravely ill. He spent an anxious night at his bedside and in the morning ran for a doctor. All day long, Juan was so preoccupied with his uncle's needs that he found no time to think of returning to our Lady for the promised sign. Before daybreak, on December 12, Juan's uncle whispered, "Go for the priest...ask him to hurry. I want to be ready to meet my God."

"Don't worry, uncle," Juan reassured. "I'll go right away!"

Juan raced on foot toward the next village to summon a priest. At the sight of Tepeyac Hill, he realized that in the excitement, he had forgotten all about fulfilling our Lady's request to return for the sign. Fearful that his uncle might die without the priest if he were detained, Juan took another road. But our Lady surprised him and stood in his way. Frightened, Juan fell on his knees and stammered, "Oh Mother Mary,...my uncle is dying. I am rushing to get a priest.... I can't stop now!"

The Lady smiled and Juan felt calm and peaceful all over. Mary spoke these reassuring words, "It will not be necessary to go for the priest, Juan, because your uncle is already completely cured. Now this is what I want you to do. Go to the top of the hill and gather all the roses that you find."

Juan scanned the top of the hill and scratched his head. There was only rock up there...never roses...but if the Lady said so, he would do it!

Mary waited as the Indian climbed the hill to find an array of Castilian roses swaying in the crisp breeze. He gathered the roses and placed them in his tilma, a sort of cloak he wore. Juan glowed with excitement. He brought the roses to our Lady who delicately rearranged them in his mantle.

"Go straight to the bishop," she told him, "and do not show anyone else but him what you are carrying."

The bishop's servants noticed that Juan was hiding something. They wanted to see his treasure. Juan answered, "What I have is only for the bishop."

One of the servants pulled an end of Juan's tilma free and spied a large red rose. He tried to reach for it, but he grabbed at thin air. How very strange.... The excited servants reported the event to the bishop who called for Juan immediately. The Indian exclaimed, "Our Lady has sent me with the sign you asked for!"

Juan opened his tilma and held out the roses. He said simply, "These are for you!"

The prelate was surprised to see them especially at that time of year but what brought the bishop and his attendants to their knees was what they saw on Juan's tilma. There...on Juan's mantle was the picture of our Lady exactly as the Indian had seen her. Juan was as surprised as they!

The bishop rose to his feet and reverently loosened the tilma from Juan's shoulder. He placed the heaven-painted picture in his chapel until the shrine requested by our Lady could be built.

News of the miracle flashed across the countryside. Missionary priests preached the event at Sunday Mass. They spoke like this, "Mary, the Mother of God, loves her children the world over. This compassion has caused her even to work miracles in behalf of those whom she loves. This is what she has done for the Aztec Indians.

"When Cortes, the Spanish invader, conquered Mexico and destroyed the pagan temples, he had hoped that the Indians would be quickly converted to Christianity. As we know, this was not the case. When they were told of God and the Mother of God, the majority of Indians shrugged their shoulders in doubt or disbelief. Very few accepted. But now all that is changed. Our Lady has shown a personal love for the Aztecs by appearing to Juan Diego."

Pilgrims brought more pilgrims to see the miraculous tilma—Juan Diego's mantle. So many people came that the bishop had to place it in the cathedral in Mexico City for veneration.

But the Indians were not satisfied with that arrangement. Volunteer laborers worked swiftly and well to construct an adobe chapel at Tepeyac. Amid great solemnity, Juan's tilma was brought there. Eventually, a magnificent shrine would be built to honor their Mother. Our Lady of Guadalupe they called her.

The Indians were in a "fiesta" mood. They danced for hours to honor their new Mother. In between, they would beg the missionary priests, "Tell us the story of our Mother again...."

"Tell us about Juan and his tilma."

"Tell us about the holy Virgin."

"We want to hear about the roses on the hill...."

The Indians were convinced that the beautiful Lady loved them. She was their Mother; she was their Lady.

Her miraculous image seemed to radiate the splendors of the true Faith, and in a few short years, the whole of Mexico became Christian.

Through the centuries, the shrine at Tepeyac has grown in size and splendor. Today it is a massive and beautiful basilica. And even now, over 450 years later, the painting is as vivid and beautiful as it was on the day that Juan showed it to the bishop.

Our Lady of Guadalupe, pray for us!

O Virgin of Guadalupe, be our Mother, too!

Mary, the Mother of God, loves her children the world over.

5

what
can
I give
to a
God
who
has
everything?

Evening had already settled on the city of Lima, Peru. There was a sudden commotion in the home of Gaspar Flores, one of the city's officials, as his wife Maria discovered that supper was not ready.

"Marianna, Marianna...where are you? Why aren't you preparing supper?"

Maria Flores opened the kitchen window that overlooked the family garden. She motioned to Marianna, the Indian servant girl who stood at the gate.

"Come in now. What are you doing out there at this hour?"

Marianna hesitated and then spoke, "It's Miss Rose, Señora. She heard the cry of someone in pain, and went to see if she could help."

"Out on the street?" the anxious mother asked. "What is that girl thinking of?"

She was about to slam the window shut and go down to the garden herself, when she saw the front gate swing slowly open. A young girl's voice called to her:

"It's all right, Mother. This poor woman was alone, and she slipped and fell on the walk. Her knee is badly hurt."

"But..."

"She's cold...and hungry, too, Mother. Can't we help her?"

Rose's gentle pleading muted her mother's objections. How could she refuse? Rose was always helping someone, either with food or clothing, not to mention all the prayers and little sacrifices she offered daily. Mama Flores sighed:

"Ah, well...yes, bring her in. At least we can give her a good meal."

Mama mumbled to herself, "What a pity. Rose is such a beautiful girl, but she won't even think of marriage. All she worries about is those ragged Indians. Perhaps she'll change her mind some day...."

Born in 1586, one of the youngest of the eleven Flores children, Rose was rather special. She had a modesty and charm that won the hearts of friends and relatives alike, and her mother had looked forward with pleasure to a good marriage for her daughter.

But Rose had other interests. She had been greatly impressed by an incident that happened on her Confirmation day. She and two other children were confirmed in the parish church of a small mountain village outside of Lima. Most of the villagers were Indians who were still a long way from being Christianized. The cruelty of some of the Spanish soldiers who had overrun and conquered the land caused the majority of the Indians to distrust anything that came from Spain, including the Faith which the missionaries preached.

When the Confirmation ceremony was over, Rose and her mother left the church. A group of Indians gathered around them in the plaza. They began to shout angrily:

"Look at the Christians!"

"They think their God is in that church!"

"Fools!"

Hearing the uproar, the archbishop had come to the church door. He had tried to calm the crowd, but they jeered and shook their fists at him. Finally Rose and Señora Flores fearfully made their way around the edge of the crowd and headed toward home. Rose never forgot that day! She explained to her mother:

"God inspired me to do something for the souls of those Indians.... I want to share with them the treasure of my faith."

"But how?" Mama asked.

"I can pray, and offer my whole day, every day, to God for their intentions. I can be patient about little troubles and ask Jesus to help these poor people."

Little by little as the days, weeks and months passed by, Rose grew in union with God, in her love for Him and for His people. She realized more and more how much the Indians suffered materially and spiritually. And so, for the love of them, she increased her penances, fasting and rising at night to pray. At the same time she kept herself busy and useful at home, especially by growing fruit and flowers which Marianna, the Indian servant, sold at the market.

Mama Flores was getting impatient again. She wanted to distract her pretty young daughter from the life of hard work and prayer to which she was devoting herself. The anxious mother often invited friends to come for a visit and then she would ask Rose to sing and play her guitar. Mama would call, "Rose, come and join us!"

Although Rose enjoyed their company and wanted to please her mother by entertaining them, she always felt attracted to a more hidden life. As she explained one day to one of her closest friends, Doña Maria de Quinones, "Mother doesn't seem to understand that I don't care about pretty dresses and having a good time. Jesus has taught me how much He loves each person and He wants me to help Him save them."

"Well, dear, why don't you become a religious?"

Rose's eyes sparkled with joy as she replied, "I've thought about that, Doña Maria. Ever since I read about the life of St. Catherine of Siena, I've wanted to be a Dominican Tertiary, too, just like her."

Doña Maria shook her head and whispered, "That is a difficult life, child. It takes a very special grace."

"You are right, Doña Maria. I've prayed and asked God to help me find out what His will is for me. Right now I believe that this is it."

"Well, we'll see," Doña Maria replied.

When she was twenty, Rose obtained her father's permission to care for some of the city's many poor women who were ill and homeless. A section of the Flores home was set apart for this purpose, and it soon came to be called "the Infirmary."

Drawn by Rose's kindness and genuine concern, more and more women came to this new infirmary. Mama Flores sometimes lost her temper over the number of "patients," and she would complain, "At her age! She should be thinking of marriage. It's a shame!"

Her husband would defend his daughter, "Now, Maria. Keep calm. You know that Rose has told us she intends never to marry!"

"Well, what is she going to do...?"

That was a good question! Just a few weeks later, on August 10, Rose Flores joined the Dominican Order as a

Tertiary and received the longed-for religious habit. Although the circumstance and routine of her life had not changed, a change was taking place within her. Her thirst for souls and her love for solitude, prayer and sacrifice grew daily. The great interior peace and joy which she felt were reflected even on her face and in her actions. She had wanted for such a long time to give her life more completely to Jesus, for His service.

On Palm Sunday of the following year, our Lord gave Rose a special sign that He had accepted her generous gift. After the procession of the palms, Rose was kneeling in prayer. She gazed at the statue of the Madonna and Child. Suddenly, right before the girl's eyes, our Lady smiled and turned toward the Infant in her arms. These words of Jesus Himself sounded in the depths of the girl's soul:

"Rose, be my spouse!"

The young tertiary could hardly contain her joy! From that day on these words echoed in her soul and she carried the treasured memory with her always. She increased the number and severity of her penances, cutting down sleep to two hours a night and fasting for long periods at a time.

Finally, when the young Dominican asked her parents' permission to live in a little hut in the garden, Mama Flores threw up her hands in despair and exclaimed to her husband, "I've tried threats...pleading and tears to persuade Rose to cut down on her fasting and to take better care of her health. She always listens so respectfully, but...."

Mr. Flores stared at the floor in silence as Rose answered her mother:

"Mother, I know that you are concerned for me. But...this is the best way for me to please God and to help my brothers and sisters in Christ. Please let me continue."

And her mother always had to give in. But the hard life which she had freely chosen began to affect her health. She became pale and very thin. When she was just twenty-nine, her physical condition caused her confessor much concern and he placed her under obedience to go and live with her friend, Doña Maria. Rose accepted this new sacrifice with her characteristic cheerfulness even though it was difficult to leave her family and her little garden cell. In Doña Maria's home she made herself as useful as she could, sewing, doing housework, caring for the younger children, even though her friend kept reminding Rose that she was a welcome guest.

Though Rose's health did improve, she knew that she would not live much longer. Shortly before her death she confided to Doña Maria, "Our Lord let me know that I will die soon,...on August 24, St. Bartholomew's feast."

On the night of August 1, Rose began the last and most painful part of her offering to the Lord. She lay dying of an incurable illness. Even breathing became almost impossible. Doña Maria and her family called in priests and doctors whom Rose knew. The young woman smiled weakly as she saw the efforts made to ease her mounting sufferings.

On the eve of August 24, she asked to see her parents. Rose whispered in her same sweet way, "I want to say good-bye. And I want to ask forgiveness of everyone for whom I may have caused trouble."

Many visitors came to see Rose throughout the day. Many of them had been befriended, helped and encouraged by her. Others had heard rumors of her years of intense prayer and sacrifice. They hoped to get a glimpse of "the young saint" as she was being called.

The hours ticked away. It was almost midnight. Rose looked around at the people still gathered in the room who were praying and watching. She whispered with a smile: "Please don't be sad that I am leaving you.... This is really such a happy day."

Her mother was at her bedside, weeping. She kept mumbling over and over: "Rose, forgive me, I should have tried to understand you better. Forgive me, child."

After a few moments of silence, Rose lifted a crucifix to her lips and whispered, "Jesus, be with me...."

A thrill of suspense raced through all those in the room. Mama Flores dried her eyes. Then she stood and stared at her daughter.

"It's all over.... It's all over. My little girl has gone to heaven."

Rose of Lima died at the age of 31. She has left us an example of heroic virtue practiced in an ordinary family situation. Her life might well be a testimony of these words of Pope Paul VI:

"Blessed are you who have realized that true Christian life calls for great courage. We cannot be Christians unless we have courage and strength. Ours must not be a half-hearted Christianity...a Christianity that seeks to avoid the hardships of sacrifices and pursues a life of comfort, honors, tranquility and pleasure. True Christianity knows all the sweetness of the style of goodness and charity but in itself is a strong, austere way."

6

giant
of
faith

On October 25, 1626, Jean de Brebeuf stepped into a Huron canoe and set out on his first mission into the uncharted wilderness of the Great Lakes region.

Although he could not speak one word of their language, an immediate feeling of kinship developed between the Red Men and this French Jesuit. Brebeuf was a man of towering stature and powerful physique, of happy disposition and patient endurance. Unlike most of the other Frenchmen that they had come in contact with, Brebeuf and the Indians could easily relate with each other. His quick adaptation to their lifestyle commanded their respect and trust.

Nonetheless, the first days were difficult. The long journey by canoe and on foot was not easy for the thirty-three-year-old priest who was accustomed to the refined life-style of French nobility.

Born in France on March 25, 1593, almost nothing is known of Brebeuf's early years until his entrance into the

Society of Jesus at the age of twenty-four. He distinguished himself in the practice of obedience: "I would rather be ground to powder than break a single rule." Such determination would later steel him against the relentless hardships of New France. Even the Indians recognized in him a man who would not break under any physical or mental torture.

After seven years in the Society of Jesus, he volunteered for missionary work in the New World. His offer was accepted and he left France in April of 1625.

Now, a little over a year after that departure, he was making his final break with the civilized world of seventeenth-century Quebec. His destination? Brebeuf was not certain. It was somewhere in the wilds of Huronia—there were no maps—Brebeuf could only trust the Indians.

He wrote vividly of his first experience:

"When rapids or torrents are reached, it is necessary to land and carry on shoulder, through woods or over high and troublesome rocks, all the baggage and the canoes themselves.... In some places, where the current is stronger than the rapids, although easier at first, the Indians get into the water and haul and guide their canoes by hand with extreme difficulty and danger; for sometimes they themselves get in up to the neck and are compelled to let go their hold, saving themselves as best they can from the rapidity of the water which snatches their canoe from them and bears it off. I kept count of the number of portages and found that we carried our canoes thirty-five times, and dragged them at least fifty."

It was during this journey that Brebeuf proved his ability to adapt to Indian customs. He helped paddle, was cheerful, never got sick, and managed to carry heavy packs. The Indians took note of this and named him "Echon" or "the-man-who-carries-loads." They meant it as a title of rare distinction.

The Indians finally put in at the village of Toanche, Brebeuf's first mission. It was a small cluster of long-houses ranging in length from twenty to eighty feet, and housing anywhere from six to twenty families.

If traveling had been difficult, accustoming himself to the routine of life in the village was even more grueling: blinding, gagging smoke from perpetual fires, stinking, decaying food and unwashed bodies, continual lack of privacy, screaming squaws and children, howling dogs, scurrying rats and mice, biting fleas and lice.... This was life in Toanche.

Despite all this, Brebeuf marveled at the Hurons' hospitality. "They never close their door to a stranger, and once having received him, they share with him the best of what they have and never send him away. When he leaves of his own accord, he pays his debt with a simple 'Thank you.' " This was providential because Brebeuf had no permanent quarters as yet. He was free to stay in any cabin, share anyone's food and remain with any family for as long as he wished.

During the first months Brebeuf acquainted himself with the Huron language and studied their customs and beliefs. Meanwhile, he and his Jesuit companion built a cabin for themselves on the outskirts of Toanche. There they would be able to pray in peace and try, as best they could, to lead a more civilized existence.

Before the Indians could be evangelized, it was necessary for Father Brebeuf to come to terms with them regarding some of their beliefs. For instance, dreams were the ruling power in their lives. Brebeuf wrote, "A dream prescribes the feasts, the songs, the games.... In a word, the dream is to be regarded as the chief god of the Hurons."

Their witchdoctors were another serious obstacle to Brebeuf's work. They all but tyrannized the people. Weather predictions, prophecies, the cure of the sick:

their pretenses were outlandish. Remedies prescribed for various illnesses were not even slightly connected with the diseases. These remedies were not only a threat to the physical health, but even the sanity of their poor victims.

When the Blackrobes appeared on the scene with simple but more humane remedies like broth, rest and quiet, it was obvious that the witchdoctors would soon be out of a job.

So it was that good Father Brebeuf began to win the hearts of his copper-skinned children. It was to be a long up-hill struggle, but, nonetheless, it *was* a beginning.

Brebeuf's secret? He was no less a giant in the spiritual life than he was in physical stature. His faith and prayer commanded God. The Indians could dance, sing, beat drums and scream hysterically in a vain effort to arouse the Great Thunder Bird to send down rain. Brebeuf, instead, could simply look up to the heavens, pray, make a sign of the cross and within a matter of minutes, the dry, parched earth was soft and moist.

Brebeuf had other qualities, too. He was quick to master the Huron tongue and, before long, he translated the basic Christian prayers into that strange, intriguing language. More than that, he managed to set what seemed to be nothing other than monosyllables and grunts, into written form, thus producing for himself and for those to follow a Huron grammar. Because of his practicality, he made tremendous inroads among the people of the great Huron nation. Had it not been for the savage Iroquois who a short time after Brebeuf's death all but erased the Huron name from the annals of history, it is believed that the entire population of Huronia would have been Christianized.

The Hurons were a peace-loving, gentle people and in spite of their often barbaric traits, Brebeuf capitalized on what was best in them with amazing success.

Perhaps the initial progress made by Brebeuf and his companion was helped in no small part by the great-hearted Champlain whom the Indians revered. In first introducing the missionaries to the Huron chiefs, Champlain had told them: "These are our fathers. We love them more than we love ourselves. The whole French nation honors them. They do not go among you for furs. They have left their friends and their country to show you the way to heaven. If you love the French as you say you do, then love and honor these our fathers."

Since the language of love is universal, the Indians understood immediately. Thus, Father Brebeuf labored for years among them before there was any thought of taking a much-needed rest. It was with nostalgia that Brebeuf returned to Quebec to recuperate from a fall which had broken his collarbone.

But while his body was in Quebec, his heart and thoughts were in Huronia. News had reached him that the Iroquois, now well-equipped with firearms sold to them by the Dutch, were attacking poorly armed Hurons.

Within three months, Brebeuf was on his way back through the vast expanses of virgin forests. He refused to leave his children orphaned.

He took up his heavy schedule of preaching, teaching and ministering to the sick. Day after day, in heat and in cold, he trudged from village to village. Soon enough the days turned into months and the months into years.

The main mission of Sainte Marie was now a well-staffed and flourishing Christian settlement. Smaller villages grew up in the neighboring woodlands. The superior of the community wrote with great satisfaction that the Indians flocked to the main settlement on Saturday evening and camped near the Fathers' house in order to attend Mass on Sunday. Even other friendly tribes, like the Algonquins, camped nearby and it was "a sweet anthem to hear the praise of God sung in three or four different languages at the same time. It is a house of peace."

But peace was a luxury in Huronia. Soon enough the Iroquois were harassing their age-long enemies with redoubled fury. In late autumn of 1648 more than three hundred Hurons were massacred by a band of Iroquois.

It was decided that more heavily fortified villages were needed. By March of 1649, with the help of Brebeuf, the Hurons were safely tucked away behind tall, heavy palisades with look-out towers and posted sentries.

One morning in early spring, Brebeuf left Sainte Marie and trekked through the melting snow to the mission of St. Louis. He spent a day and a night there. Meanwhile, only three miles away, the village of St. Ignace slept peacefully within its unguarded and unlocked palisades.

Wielding tomahawks and muskets, Iroquois smeared with war paint, slowly and stealthily darted from tree to tree until they reached the clearing around St. Ignace. In a matter of minutes, one thousand warriors descended on the village and its inhabitants reducing everything to charred ruins.

Three Hurons managed to escape and flee to the mission of St. Louis where they roused Brebeuf and the other villagers. "The Iroquois are coming! They are almost at your gates!"

Most of the able-bodied people ran for their lives, leaving only the Jesuits and about eighty braves to defend the settlement.

The sound of whoops and shrieks grew louder. Soon arrows buzzed through the air and gunshots vibrated through the forest. The Iroquois swarmed around the palisades and cut through with their hatchets. Brebeuf and his companions were taken captive and led back to what was left of St. Ignace. Here the Iroquois set up torture posts with fires burning around the captives. Before

Brebeuf took up his heavy schedule of preaching, teaching and ministering to the sick. Day after day, in heat and cold, he trudged from village to village.

tying Brebeuf to one of the posts, they pounced on him, ripped out his fingernails, broke the bones in his hands and began munching on his fingers.

Because of his physical stature, they wreaked their worst cruelties on him with the hope that he would break down and plead for mercy.

They held firebrands to his skin until it sizzled; then they slashed him with knives. But Brebeuf only encouraged his Huron converts to remain strong. To this, one of the Hurons replied, "Echon, our thoughts will be in heaven while our bodies suffer on earth. Pray to God for us and ask Him to show us mercy. We will invoke Him until we die."

New torments were tried. But above it all was the calm voice of Brebeuf who kept repeating, "My Jesus, have mercy on us!" His tall form was still erect. This only infuriated the Iroquois. His lower lip was cut off and red-hot irons were thrust down his throat. Brebeuf did not flinch. They cut strips of flesh from his arms and legs and ate it in front of him.

A renegade Huron poked fun: "You told us that the more one suffers on earth, the happier he will be in heaven. We want to make you very happy. We are tormenting you because we love you. You should thank us."

Since this only evoked another prayer, they cut off his nose, upper lip, and a piece of his tongue. Then they gouged out his eyes. Brebeuf's physical stamina weakened as they hacked off his charred feet. Finally they tore off his scalp and cut out his heart. In true warrior style they devoured it and drank his blood. If nothing else, this was a tribute of honor to his steadfast courage.

Not long after, the Iroquois, suspecting a large band of Hurons to be coming against them, fled in panic into the woods, leaving behind them the mutilated body of Father John de Brebeuf.

Three days later a Jesuit priest and some French settlers, along with Huron guides, came and recovered his body. They carried it back to the mission of St. Marie where it was cleansed and clothed in priestly vestments and placed in a wooden casket.

When Brebeuf had first set foot in Huronia twenty-three years before, there had not been a single Christian in the whole territory. Now there were nearly seven thousand baptized Christians.

His superior wrote the sad but glorious news to his Jesuit brothers in France: "Father Jean de Brebeuf had been chosen by God to be the first apostle of the Hurons, the first of our Society to set foot there. Not having found a single person there who invoked the name of God, he labored so successfully for their salvation that before his death he had the consolation of seeing the cross of Jesus Christ planted everywhere with glory and adored in a country which from the birth of the world had never been Christian."

7

"woman who who prays always"

"Come back here, you silly thing!" cried out a laughing Philippine Duchesne. The little boy squealed with delight as his eighteen-year-old sister caught up with him and swung him high in the air, setting him down gently.

"Do it again! Do it again! Bet you can't catch me!" he cried as he ran around the family courtyard.

The gleeful screams of his little son and the deeper laughter of his beloved daughter brought Pierre-Francois Duchesne to the window overlooking the courtyard. He smiled as he watched his children play. "What am I going to do with you, Rose Philippine?" he silently asked. "What am I going to do without you?" She looked so happy when she played with the children or instructed them, or even just helped her mother around the house. "It wouldn't be so bad if she wanted to get married," he thought. "Then she could come and visit often and even bring little grandchildren to sit on my knee and tell me of their childish adventures. But, no! She wants to be a nun!"

At first Monsieur Duchesne had been violently opposed to his daughter's entering the convent, but his love for Philippine had eventually softened his will. "So Christ has called you?" he mused. "And you've pledged yourself to His service and love? How could I refuse you your dearest wish? But not yet, I can't let you go yet." He was brought back to the present when Philippine saw him at the window and waved. And somehow in that instant he sensed with sadness that he would not be able to keep her at home much longer.

On a beautiful warm day in 1788 Philippine Duchesne and her aunt walked up the hill to the convent of Sainte-Marie. Philippine, who had attended school at Sainte-Marie for several years, felt the need to talk to Mother de Murinais about entering the Visitation cloister. Her Aunt Perier was happy to accompany her, not realizing, however, how the visit would end. The interview with Mother de Murinais started out in a normal manner; the sister had often conversed with Philippine about religious life. But suddenly Philippine announced, "I am here at Sainte-Marie and I know it is God's will for me to be here." Turning to Mother Murinais, she added, "If you will accept me as a postulant, I will remain here now with the Visitation Nuns."

"You can't be serious!" exclaimed Aunt Perier, stiffening on the edge of her chair. "You haven't given this enough thought!" She looked expectantly at Mother de Murinais. "Surely you won't consider letting her stay here without her parents' permission!" Receiving no answer, the concerned aunt again turned to Philippine. "How could you ever think of such a thing?" she asked reproachfully.

Philippine answered quietly, "You know I have thought of little else for years."

"But how could you leave your family without even saying goodbye? What will your poor mother and father say?"

Philippine became silent and Aunt Perier tried another approach. "Please come home with me, Philippine. We can all talk this over calmly when we get home. Please," she implored.

Philippine turned pleading eyes toward Mother de Murinais. After a pause that seemed very long to both Philippine and Aunt Perier, the mother superior answered, "She will remain here with us."

Aunt Perier stood up weakly and allowed herself to be shown to the door. Perhaps she—who had been one of Philippine's closest friends—really understood why her niece had decided to enter the convent in this manner. Philippine loved her family too intensely to be able to make the break in any other way.

A few days later Madame and Monsieur Duchesne and Philippine's baby sister Melanie made their way up the hill to Sainte-Marie. The meeting with Philippine was tempestuous. The young woman firmly held her ground, concealing her inner torment. Parents and daughter both suffered deeply, but Philippine knew that she could not turn back.

After her parents left, the new postulant made her way to the chapel, where she wept silently and offered her sufferings to God. She thanked Him for the grace of having persevered in her decision, and she renewed her consecration to Him, drawing peace and strength from Christ in the Blessed Sacrament, who was to sustain her in the many sacrifices she was to make throughout her long life. To her no sacrifice seemed too great to make for One who had sacrificed so much for her.

Philippine found great peace in doing her simple duties around the convent. The greatest joy, though, came from her visits to the Blessed Sacrament. She would often ask the superior if she could stay up at night for some extra prayer. This wish granted, she would sometimes remain in motionless prayer for hours. Occasionally she would become so lost in God that she would lose all consciousness of time and be found still kneeling in silent meditation when the others came into the chapel in the morning. Philippine never tired of praying at night like this, for she found her rest in God.

The young sister's joy was not to last long, however. In 1792, after only a few years in religious life, Philippine Duchesne was forced to put away her religious habit and leave her convent home. The forces of the French Revolution had ordered the closing of all convents and the disbanding of religious orders.

Philippine's heart was aching as she ran into the welcoming arms of her father. Her family was glad to have her with them again and had great sympathy for her in her sorrow. Although this understanding made her new life easier to bear, she was not content to remain idle at home.

Living with relatives or other religious who had been forced to leave their convents, Philippine Duchesne spent the next twelve years doing secret works of mercy. She ministered to the sick and dying and prepared the dead to be buried. She sheltered priests who were in hiding and led them to people who needed the sacraments. She taught neglected children. During all this time, however, she never lost sight of her religious vocation and tried always to live by the rule she had learned in the convent.

The adventure and danger of this work appealed to Philippine. She had always wanted to be a missionary and a martyr for Christ. Not a dreamer, she had no use for unreality. Rather, she dedicated herself totally to *the Reality*, who is God.

When finally the situation for religious began to improve, Philippine managed to obtain possession of the convent she had lived in and loved. It had been used as a prison by the revolutionary government.

But Philippine's attempts to permanently reunite the scattered members of her community were in vain. Gradually, God's will became clearer, and in 1804 Philippine and her few remaining companions asked to be admitted into the Society of the Sacred Heart, which had been founded four years before by the young Madeleine-Sophie Barat. Their convent was thus to become the second convent of the new congregation.

Philippine Duchesne became intensely devoted to her new spiritual mother, Mother Barat, and confided even her deepest secrets to her. Her most treasured dream was to do missionary work among the Indians in America, and she often asked this of Mother Barat. St. Madeleine-Sophie, however, always replied, "Not yet." Among other things, she was worried about Philippine's health. Philippine worked with such energy and zeal that it often took the motherly eye of her loving superior to notice her frequent illnesses and other physical sufferings. Philippine never let these slow her down, though. She continued in her strict self-imposed penances and mortifications —and she also persisted in hounding Mother Barat (and heaven) to send her to the American missions.

Meanwhile—in 1815—Philippine founded the first convent of her order in Paris.

On May 29, 1818, the Feast of the Sacred Heart, Philippine Duchesne set foot on American soil. She was forty-nine. With deep emotion, she knelt in the mire and kissed the ground, bidding her companions, "You kiss it, too." Tears of joy bathed her radiant face, as her grateful prayers rose to the Heart of Jesus.

The Indian missions—her dream—now seemed almost within her grasp. But not quite. The clergy felt that other areas were more important, so Mother Duchesne's first assignment was to found a convent and open a free school for girls at St. Charles, in what was soon to be the state of Missouri.

Over the next few years Mother Duchesne and her companions founded several convents, academies, free schools and orphanages in Missouri and Louisiana. Philippine became a tireless traveler. She became used to journeying on foot and on horseback, in a steamboat or on a raft, in a springless carriage or in a two-wheeled cart. Like all pioneers, she had to put up with cold, hunger and illness. And she also experienced opposition, ingratitude, even calumny.

In 1841, preparations were at last being made for direct mission work among the Indians. Philippine was seventy-two and had become so infirm that the sisters had decided not to include her in the next expedition. After twenty-three years of intense labor in America, her dream of the Indian missions seemed to be fading forever....

"Mother Duchesne...Mother Duchesne," a gentle voice broke her prayerful musing. "Father Verhaegen is here."

Mother Duchesne roused herself and walked slowly to the parlor to meet the kind priest. "Good morning, Father," she said and stopped for fear of the emotions that were welling up within her.

"Good morning, Mother Duchesne. It's good to see you," the priest answered warmly. "They haven't been overworking you with last-minute preparations for the trip, have they?" he asked with a twinkle in his eyes.

"No, not at all," she answered softly.

"I was planning to visit the mission this month and thought that I might escort you good sisters myself. Everything's almost ready, isn't it?"

Mother Duchesne looked at Mother Matheron and then down at her own knotted fingers clutching the rosary beads. Excitedly Mothers Matheron and Gray began to talk to Father about the trips and the preparations that had been made. Philippine sat silently by, trying to keep back the tears.

"It looks as if everything is all ready, Father," Mother Matheron concluded. "Baggage, departure time and place, steamboat reservations for three sisters...."

"Three?" Father Verhaegen asked with surprise. Suddenly he realized why Mother Duchesne had been so silent. He turned to see the tears falling unheeded down her cheeks. "Oh, but Mother Duchesne has to come also," he said gently to Mother Gray. Philippine was the one he wanted most at the mission. "Even if she cannot use both legs, she must come. Even if I have to carry her all the way, she will come. Maybe she will not be able to work much," he continued with a gentle smile, "but she will make our mission successful by her prayers. Just her presence there will bring down God's blessing on our work."

Father Verhaegen's prediction proved true, and the missionary work among the Indians was greatly blessed by Mother Duchesne's presence. She could not teach them or cook for them as the other sisters did, but she never ceased praying for them and visiting them whenever she was able to. The Potawatomi loved and respected her and brought countless gifts of fresh corn and eggs, chickens and other things to show their affection for the "good old lady," as they often called her. Sometimes while Philippine was lost in prayer before the tabernacle, devoted Indians would slip into the chapel and watch her, then silently go up to her to kneel and kiss the frayed hem of her habit or the fringe of her shawl. They lovingly called her "Woman-who-prays-always."

Philippine suffered greatly from the physical hardships and illness, but she found peace and joy in all this. Her greatest suffering came when she was told that she was to return to St. Charles after only two years at the mission. But as always, suffering only served to bring her closer to the sorrowful Heart of Jesus. In a letter to her sister she wrote, "It seems to me that in leaving the Indians I left my real element, and now I can only yearn for that land from which there will be no departure. God knows why I was recalled, and that is enough."

Mother Duchesne spent the last ten years of her life in relative obscurity in St. Charles. She was hidden, that is, from all but God. To Him she was ever-present, offering her prayers and sacrifices at His altar. In a prayer written years earlier she had said:

"O my God, I desire to live as a victim offered in a spirit of penance and love, whose perfume will rise even to the Heart of Jesus. May my *whole being* be the victim, all that I am and all that I have. May my own *heart* be the *altar*, my separation from the world and all earthly pleasures the sacrificial *knife*. May my love be the consuming *fire*, and my yearning *desires* the *breeze* that fans it. Let me pour on it the *incense* and *perfume* of all virtues, and to this mystical sacrifice let me bring *all that I cling* to, that I may offer all, burn all, consume all, keeping back nothing for self. O divine Love, my very God, accept this sacrifice which I desire to offer you at every instant of my life."

On November 18, 1852, God accepted the sacrifice of Philippine Duchesne and took her soul to the altar of His heart in heaven, to the land she had so long yearned for—the land of no departures—there to greet the many beloved souls who had gone before her and to await the arrival of the many she had helped on their heavenward journey.

"O divine Love, my very God, accept this sacrifice which I desire to offer You at every instant of my life."

8

"number
twenty-four"

France—1794—it is early May. The pleasant countryside is bathed in bright sunshine and dew sparkles on the young blades of grass. No one is aware of the tragedy about to take place. Paris alone will be witness. It is there, there in that city, that spring has not yet come.

The doors of the Conciergerie open; two or three tumbrels roll out. The riders have not seen sunlight for some time and their hands instinctively go up to shade their eyes. These people are setting out on a journey that is both short and long. They have two destinations—the first, Place de la Revolution; the second, eternity.

All of the prisoners look peaceful, but one among them is particularly serene. She is wearing a white dress and there is a certain air of dignity and modesty about her person.

The tumbrels halt for a moment and then turn into the open street. Crowds of people line the death route. Some of them are heartless, others indifferent, and still others, sympathetic. Suddenly, she is recognized. "It is the citizeness Elizabeth." They look with mixed emotions of both hate and awe. They are sending their princess to her execution.

Elizabeth looks around her. These are her people. She still loves them. She forgives them. She has compassion on them. If the sacrifice of her life is necessary for the happiness of France, then let them take it. It is all the same to her as long as some day peace and order will reign and God will once more have His rightful place. These are her thoughts now at the supreme moment of holocaust. But long before she had already made an offering of her life for her beloved France not only in her heart and words but by her life as well.

"Number twenty-four—Elizabeth Capet," a harsh voice called out across the execution site. The crowd ceased its roar of "Long live the Republic!" A reverent hush suddenly came over everyone.

Within a matter of minutes the guillotine did its job and the sacrifice was consummated. At the moment of Elizabeth's death a strong odor of roses filled the entire extent of the Place de la Revolution and the rabble quickly cleared away in fright. Was it only coincidence? Even Robespierre had misgivings about this execution.

Madame Elizabeth of France was born at the Palace of Versailles on May 3, 1764. When she was only a little over a year old, her father, the Dauphin, died. Two years later her mother, the Dauphiness Marie Josephe of Saxony, went to join her husband. Sorrow and suffering were to mark the rest of Elizabeth's short life.

Much to the dismay of her governess, the Countess of Marsan, traces of an independent, self-willed character were soon evident in Elizabeth.

By the time she was six, Elizabeth flatly refused to study the alphabet. Her excuse? Princesses who are surrounded by servants have no need to work themselves. Temper tantrums were also frequent. It was only time, patience and understanding that would mold her otherwise unruly character into one of humility, self-effacement and compassion. The loss of both parents and life at court could have had a devastating effect on Elizabeth had it not been for Madame de Mackau, her second governess, who also proved to be a second mother to her. With firm voice and firm hand Baroness de Mackau made Elizabeth understand that even princesses have duties and responsibilities that they cannot shirk. The carefree years of youth began to wane and Madame Elizabeth, the sister of Louis XVI and sister-in-law of Marie Antoinette learned early just how trying life can be.

On August 13, 1775, Madame Elizabeth was confirmed and made her first Holy Communion.

This day marked a turning point in her life. A contemporary noted that even her tone of voice changed.

Elizabeth, now eleven, endeared herself to everyone. Marie Antoinette wrote of her: "I am delighted with Elizabeth. She shows herself capable of a disarming honesty and great depth of feeling. She is a charming child, who has wit, character and much grace." The Queen took such a liking to her that she did not hesitate to frequently leave the court, retire to Elizabeth's apartment, and join her in a game of tag.

Elizabeth preferred the simple side of life. Fuss and fanfare, she believed, were only for the King and Queen. This reasoning marked her entire life. She never sought the limelight. It was not until tragedy and disgrace struck the royal family that Elizabeth came to the foreground, not to receive praise and honor, but scorn and ridicule.

By the time she reached thirteen, all sorts of stories were circulated concerning her future. "She will marry

the Infante of Portugal...." "No, I heard the Duke of
Aosta...." "Wait, Emperor Joseph II is coming to Versailles. The King must have some intentions about marrying off his younger sister. Such an alliance would be
useful to France...."

But at fifteen, she still had no intention of marrying
and neither the King nor Queen made mention of it. She
secluded herself from the court and pursued a life of
prayer, study and work. One day a lady-in-waiting remarked about Elizabeth's embroidery,

"It's a real pity you are so talented."

"Why?"

"Such fine work would be a great advantage for poor
girls. It would enable them to earn bread for themselves
and their families."

Elizabeth looked at her, smiled, and replied quite
simply, "Perhaps that's the reason God has given it to me.
Who knows if some day I may have to make use of it to
provide food for me and mine?"

Madame Elizabeth discreetly played the role of
guardian angel among the members of the entire royal
family. She tried to soothe hurt feelings, calm inevitable
disagreements, and restore and maintain peace.

On December 19, 1778, Madame Royale, the first
child of Louis XVI and Marie Antoinette was born.
Then, on October 22, 1781, the long-awaited heir was
born, the ill-fated Dauphin who would never become
king. He would die at an early age.

Madame Elizabeth carried on extensive correspondence within France and far beyond its confines. Her letters give an in-depth view of a soul completely human
but amazingly supernatural.

To one of her childhood friends, she wrote in later
life, "Friendship, you surely know, my dear, is a second
life. It sustains us in this lower world." During the last
months of her life, she wrote to an acquaintance: "Happy

is the heart of him who can feel in the greatest upheavals of this world that God is still with him. Happy are the saints who, pierced with wounds, never slacken in their praise of God at every instant of the day. Beg this grace for those who are weak and wanting in fidelity like myself."

As Madame Elizabeth passed out of her teen years, rumors spread that she was soon to enter the Carmelite Monastery of St. Denis. One day the King remarked, "Nothing pleases me more than to see you going to visit your aunt at the convent of St. Denis, but do not imitate her. Elizabeth, I need you with me."

Then and there, the young princess resolved to dedicate herself to the service of her family. She lived a life so totally detached from self-love that she barely had anything else to offer at the time of her death on the scaffold.

Elizabeth, amid the hustle and bustle of court life, found time for the common folk. It was entirely normal for the princess to leave the royal residence to bring food and clothes to poor families or to care for the sick with her own hands. She had a special knack for mixing herbs and preparing medicine for the ill. All this was not done with an air of condescension, but with complete simplicity and serenity.

Elizabeth's twenty-fifth birthday came and went, but not without notice—the first rumblings of the approaching danger were heard.

—The Meeting of the Estates General
—The Tennis Court Oath
—The Storming of the Bastille

Events such as these could hardly pass unheeded. Little by little members of the royal family and the great ones of the court dispersed. Elizabeth was counseled to leave at once. It was no longer safe at Versailles. She would go, she retorted, only when the King left. Her duty was to remain at his side, even if it meant death.

"I have no desire for martyrdom," she wrote, "but I know that I should be very glad of the assurance that I am ready to suffer it rather than abandon one article of my faith. I trust that if such is to be my destiny, God will give me the strength."

The fateful day came. On October 5th, an armed band of several thousand men and women left Paris and headed toward Versailles. Their goal? Custody of the King and Queen.

Elizabeth's ordeal had just begun.

Two days later the mob re-entered Paris with Louis XVI, Marie Antoinette, their two children and Madame Elizabeth.

They were never to see Versailles again. First, they were kept in custody at the Tuileries Palace, uninhabited since 1655.

Next, it was a prison called The Temple.

Elizabeth suffered all kinds of calumny and slander. All the worse for her, because these people had so soon forgotten her countless deeds of mercy in their behalf. She begged God for the peace and well-being of her beloved French brothers and sisters, while they plotted for her death.

During their confinement at The Temple, Elizabeth cared for the needs of the royal family to whom she had pledged her life's full measure of devotion. She spent much time in prayer and carried on a small amount of correspondence with the outside world.

Then came the first mortal blow—the execution of the King. His final words were those of a true Christian: "I die innocent of all the crimes imputed to me. I pardon those responsible for my death and I pray God that the blood which you shed this day may never be laid to the account of France."

A few months later it was the Queen's turn. She had been imprisoned in the Conciergerie, had had a mock trial and was then executed. Elizabeth, at the time of her own death, did not know of the Queen's execution and believed that she was still alive.

Shortly after Marie Antoinette's death, the decision was made to clear out all the persons imprisoned in The Temple. Elizabeth was among them. She spent the last night of her life at the infamous Conciergerie and together with twenty-three other people she was condemned to death the following day after a ridiculous hearing. In the few hours separating her trial from her execution she continually consoled those who were to die with her. "They are not asking of us," she said, "as they did of the martyrs of the past, the sacrifice of our belief. They are only demanding our miserable lives. Let us with resignation make this small sacrifice to God."

Madame Elizabeth was only thirty at the time of her death. She had never lived in the limelight; she was always hidden. Yet, she is a model of fraternal charity lived to the fullest degree. "Greater love than this no one has that he give up his life for another."

9

Margherita

"I'm sorry. I'm sorry, but there's really nothing I can do. She made up her mind a long time ago. Margherita will not marry."

All the hope in Francis' heart vanished as Margherita's father showed him to the door. Desperately he pleaded, "Will you at least tell her what I came for?" And then he told his story.

There were three in his home—his mother, himself, and his little son, Anthony. His wife had died a year before. He was working feverishly, holding two jobs, but even his meager savings had vanished in the effort to provide for his sickly mother and his son. Francis had tried, had struggled with all his might to keep his home together. But it was just too much for him. Anthony, once lively and happy, had grown sullen and selfish. The house was a wreck, and the grandmother was too sick to help. He needed a wife. And Anthony needed a mother.

Touched, with his eyes full of pity, Margherita's father promised to speak on Francis' behalf. Yes, Margherita already knew of his plight. And, well, he, her father, would do what he could.

Downhearted, Francis retraced his steps, stopping only to send up a heartsick prayer for guidance and help. It seemed as if every door were closed. He was so wretchedly poor. What young woman in her right mind would consider such a proposal? An old, invalid mother-in-law, a problem child, and little reassurance that things would get better. Who would accept such a proposal?

Margherita's father let his wife in on the problem, and together they spoke with their daughter. What they said that night no one will ever know, but she accepted. On June 6, 1812, Margherita Occhiena, twenty-four, would marry Francis Bosco, twenty-eight. She knew well the challenge that awaited her.

"Welcome to your new home, Margherita."

"Thank you. Thank you so much, Nonnina."

Margherita embraced her new mother-in-law and stepped across the threshold. This small farm house, one of eight in the tiny hamlet of Becchi in Northern Italy, would be her new home. With a smile she realized that Francis had repainted the house to make it cheerful and homey again. What it really needed was a mother. And she had come to be just that.

It was a difficult task, being the mother of that family. Margherita worked hard, cooking and cleaning and taking care of the home. Though seventy-eight-year-old Nonnina could scarcely move and needed constant attention, she and Margherita grew to be fast friends. Nonnina must have been annoying at times, yet Margherita made no sign of it. She always treated her mother-in-law with great respect and affection, and often went to her for advice and a friendly chat.

Time flew fast, and weeks turned into months. The Bosco family was happy, although very poor. Francis worked hard, but when he was on the way home from work his heart would sing at the thought of his capable little wife waiting for him. She would have supper on the fire, as he always knew from the smoke curling from the chimney. Once inside the door he'd embrace her, and laughing, they would run together to the fire to see the surprise she had cooked up.

One happy day a new member was added to the family. Margherita bore a son—Joseph. He was named in honor of the great saint who proved himself a provider and special friend of the family. Not long after, another boy was born—John. Both boys had very good dispositions. Joseph was meek and always happy. And John stole every heart with his playful cheerfulness. Margherita loved them both fiercely. And Anthony, her step-son, held the same place in her heart. No distinction was ever made between him and his two half-brothers.

One scorching day Francis toiled hard in the fields. His eyes squinted in the beating sun, while the perspiration ran from his body and drenched his clothes. Finally, finally, it was time to go home. Home! The habitual happiness swelled his heart as he thought of the lovely Margherita awaiting him. What a happy home she had made it! Suddenly his employer appeared and mentioned that one barrel of wine in the cellar seemed to be going bad. Could he bottle it before going home? Francis winced, but quickly reassured him that he would. Margherita would have to wait a little longer tonight.

Never one to complain or shirk his work, Francis went to the wine cellar at once. It was cold and clammy, but he paid no attention. For several more hours he pushed his exhausted and overheated body, emptying the wine barrel into bottles. By the time he was finished, he could scarcely drag himself out and home. Anxious Margherita realized that he was too sick even to eat. Francis went straight to bed.

During the night a high fever seized Francis, and violent chills shook his weakened body. By the time dawn appeared the sick man could not leave his bed. Frantic,

Margherita at once called for the doctor who lived in another town. He hurried, realizing the urgency of the case, but by the time he reached the Bosco home, he could only shake his head slowly. Though Francis was a young man, in the prime of life, there was no hope. He could not last much longer. He had pneumonia.

Margherita's heart sank and her lips trembled. Could it be possible that Francis would really die? Could he die now, when their home was so happy? She sobbed. Why, oh why? She loved him so much, and the three children needed him. He had needed a wife, and after only five years of marriage—a delightfully happy marriage—he was dying. Was it possible?

As the priest performed the last rites, Margherita struggled to control herself and accept God's will. Seeing her sorrowful eyes turned on him, Francis murmured, "Margherita, don't mourn for me.... See how good God is. Since I must die, it is He who comes in person to take me to Himself. It's Friday, the very day of the week on which our Redeemer Himself died on the cross for us. You mustn't cry, you mustn't mourn."

Margherita tried to smile at him, but her heart beat painfully and her eyes threatened to overflow. The room grew silent, very silent. Only the labored breathing of the dying man could be heard. Francis finally reopened his eyes to see his wife still standing beside his bed and said softly, "Have faith in God, great faith. Believe in Him; trust Him completely. Remember always that I entrust *all* our dear children to you, but very, very especially I entrust to your care our baby, our youngest, our dear little John. Take good care of him for me."

Those were Francis' last words. Serenely, confidently, his soul returned to its Maker and confided to His special protection the care of his grieving family.

It seemed as though Francis' peace had spread to his wife. He looked so beautiful that she wanted the youngest, John, to see him like this for the last time. She ran down to fetch the two-year-old and he toddled up the steep stairs after her.

"See how beautiful he is?" pointed out Margherita. Her voice trembled as she spoke. Little John promptly climbed onto the bed beside the father he loved so passionately. Thinking that Daddy's stillness was caused by sleep, he resolved to remain there until his father awoke. But Margherita had other ideas.

"Come on, John. Come back downstairs now."

Bellowing a protest, John clung to the lifeless body beside him. Why did Mother want to leave so soon? Why, he had just gotten there!

"If Daddy no go, John no go."

And his little fists clenched in determination.

Margherita could stand it no more. Bursting into tears, she sobbed, "Poor, poor little John! You no longer have a father. Daddy is dead!" These words John would remember for the rest of his life.

After the funeral Margherita began to pick up the pieces of her shattered family. Now she had to be not only the mother, but also the father.

The courage and faith that had enabled Margherita to accept the challenge of her marriage in the beginning came to the fore again. Only time would be able to heal the wound of sorrow that Francis' death had caused, but Margherita did not forget her duties in the meantime. She went to work in the fields alongside her sons. Together they worked. Together they prayed.

But new problems arose. As though the struggle to be well enough fed and clothed were not enough, Anthony began making trouble. He wanted to be the boss since he was the eldest boy, and asserted his authority by being cruel to his brothers. Many times would Margherita sigh in discouragement at his behavior. She prayed—oh, how hard she prayed—that Anthony would see the hardships he was causing for the rest of the family. But she did more than just pray. No chance was lost to gently convince him of his error.

One night as they said their prayers together, Margherita resolved to be firm.

"Give us this day our daily bread, and forgive us our trespasses...." At this point of the Our Father, she turned to Anthony and declared, "You may as well not say this part. You know you don't mean it."

Taken by surprise, Anthony retorted, "Who will stop me if I want to say it?"

Eyes flashing, Margherita replied, "I will. You've been unbearable with your brothers all day. They are helpless against your cruelty."

Anthony remained silent during the rest of the night prayers. When the others finished he jumped up and cried, "I'm sorry, Mamma! I'll never be so mean again." He really meant to try, but somehow he just wasn't able to control himself.

Anthony loved the farm passionately. He was proud of his own exceptional strength and physical ability. To him, learning was a waste of time, even presumption on the part of such poor peasants as they were. All his energies were spent in efforts to farm better, to produce more. Certainly it was hard work, very hard work. But he loved it.

In his farming efforts, Anthony pushed his younger brothers hard. At times they seemed so reluctant to do what he told them. Especially John. He had somehow gotten it into his head that he didn't want to be a farmer, that he wanted to be a priest. Anthony could not see this. He grew jealous and bitter against John, and used every opportunity to ridicule and oppose his priestly dream.

Sensitive John resented the harsh treatment, but realized that the best way to handle the situation was to offer no resistance. He tried always to obey Anthony and never contradict him. At times he was even able to make a joke out of an insult aimed at him, and this made the strained relations a little more bearable.

Margherita suffered tremendously at the bitterness among her boys. She tried hard to keep peace, and help Anthony to be more reasonable. Sometimes it seemed a hopeless task. At other times it seemed they were making headway.

Eventually, through much prayer and gentle firmness, Margherita was able to smooth the way for John to accomplish his dream. At the first Mass he said when his family could be present, Margherita, Joseph and Anthony knelt together. Afterwards, Anthony knelt to receive his brother's blessing. Through Margherita's prayers and efforts, her children were reconciled.

In all her troubles Margherita never wavered. Remembering the last request of her beloved husband, she had always striven to bring up her children well. She wanted them to become real men, who would be able to take their places in society and live uprightly. And through her prayers and constant efforts, she was able to fulfill Francis' dying wish. Anthony settled down as a good father of his own home. Joseph, too, got married and lived a wholesome life. John became a holy priest, famous for his work with young boys. Margherita helped him in his work, becoming a mother all over again to countless boys who were abandoned and homeless. She cooked for them, sewed for them and helped them in their personal problems. John would be forever grateful for this, and for the way she had molded his own character and spiritual life. In fact, she did such a good job that today John is called "saint"—St. John Bosco.

10

cloth
and
tailor....

"Good night, Father Cugliero."

"Good night, John, good night, Tony,...just one minute, Dominic. Wait until the others leave. I want to talk to you."

Dominic Savio's knees turned to water. He hadn't done anything wrong that he knew of. When the last of the boys had left, Father Cugliero walked up to the boy. He put his big hand on Dominic's shoulder, and asked:

"I'm your pastor, you know, and I've been thinking about you. Say, what are you planning to be when you grow up?"

"A priest."

"Oh? A new idea of yours? When did you first start thinking about it?"

"Well,...there wasn't a time when I *first* started thinking about it. I've always wanted to be a priest!... Of course, I know it takes a lot of money and a good education. That's going to be hard, but God will figure out a way if I try my best."

"Naturally, *God* will figure it out!... And I'm going to help Him a little."

A few days later, Father Cugliero was alone in his room opening his mail. All the while Dominic Savio was in the back of his mind. He deserved the chance to pursue that vocation which is such a great gift of God's love. The priest asked himself out loud:

"What am I going to do for Dominic?"

The priest opened the next letter. It was from his friend, the famed Don Bosco, who would one day be St. John Bosco.

"Don Bosco, of course, I should have thought of it sooner. Dominic can go to Don Bosco's Oratory. What better place than with this great priest to begin his quest for the priesthood?"

Father Cugliero put on his cape and broad-rimmed hat and caught the next coach out of town. He was on his way to Turin, Italy, Father John Bosco's home-base!

The coach came to a rude halt. Father Cugliero stepped out onto solid earth again. His footsteps were long and quick. He knew just where he was going. Where else but to see Don Bosco! Stepping up to the front door of the Oratory, the priest banged loudly. A plump, smiling woman answered. She greeted him warmly and beckoned him into the parlor. Everyone in North Italy knew Mama Margherita, the mother of Don Bosco. In a few minutes she was back with something hot to drink; then she slipped away again.

Don Bosco came in a few minutes later, moving quickly as usual. He wore that perpetual smile of his which was so sincere, so real. Affability seemed to be his trademark. What was this priest's apostolate? Boys! Especially the poor, the neglected, the overlooked. He wanted to give them a chance—in fact, every chance—to become useful citizens for this life and the next.

The first boys who had come to him had slept on piles of straw. Mama Margherita had walked from one to the other, snuggling them in and offering words of comfort. Now those days of extreme want were gone forever. Don Bosco found jobs for the older boys as apprentices for various trades and sent the young ones to school. His program also allowed for ordinary boys from fine families. They were sent out to the best of schools run by friends of the beloved priest. His "boys" were admitted free. So while they lived at the Oratory, they went to school. Such would be the case of Dominic Savio.

"I tell you, Don Bosco, he's another St. Aloysius!"

"Who?"

"Why, Dominic Savio, of course! He's the boy I've come here to ask you to admit to the Oratory. Father, please give him a chance!"

"I'm sure you're right, Father. On October 7, I'll be in my hometown, Becchi. That's so near Mondonio. Bring the boy to meet me!"

Back in Mondonio, Father Cugliero and Dominic had a little talk.

"Ever hear of Don Bosco?"

"Sure, who hasn't?"

"Would you like to go to his school in Turin?"

"Would I!... Oh, but I'll bet it costs a lot of money."

"Money's no drawback when it comes to the things of God. Faith is what you need. And that is a rarer quality than any amount of money. So you want to go to Don Bosco's school?"

"Oh, yes!"

"Then you're going!"

Don Bosco arrived at Becchi on schedule—Sunday, October 1, 1854. The news flashed across the countryside. Dominic ran to tell his dad, Charles Savio, the village blacksmith. Mr. Savio was genuinely grateful for this wonderful opportunity for his son. He believed that the interview with Don Bosco would be successful. Naturally he was proud of his son—what father isn't? Life would have been much easier for the blacksmith if his oldest son had chosen to stay home and help, but this sacrifice was small when compared to the honor of having his son a priest.

"You're sure about this, aren't you, son?"

"Dead sure!"

"Good, good! Mom and I will back you up all the way. Tomorrow morning we'll go to Becchi."

The village blacksmith was dressed in his best and Dominic almost sparkled. Together they made the brief journey to Becchi. As the Bosco family home came into view, Dominic's knees grew very weak, just as they had on every other momentous occasion of his short life. His cheeks flushed red and he could feel the perspiration forming on his hands. It wasn't bad enough that in a few minutes he was going to be meeting a "living saint," but then, his whole future would depend upon that meeting. When this thought struck, his knees began to shake as well. They walked across the front porch and Mr. Savio knocked on the door. It opened and a youthful, dark-haired priest answered.

"Good morning!... Come in.... My name is Don Bosco!"

"Father Cugliero told you about me, Don Bosco. How I want very much to come to your Oratory!"

"Oh yes, I didn't forget. In fact, I said to myself: 'If the boy's as eager as Father Cugliero is, he should be coming for the interview first thing Monday morning.' "

"Y...You mean you knew it was me when we knocked on the door a few minutes ago?"

"How are your school marks, son?"

"Fine, Father, at least I think so. I know I can always do better. You see, I want very much to become a priest. I promise to study hard and to do everything you tell me."

The conversation continued without effort. The priest and the boy were completely in each other's confidence. There would not be a "get acquainted period" for either of them. It was as if they had always known each other.

Dominic got up and walked over to the priest's chair. He put his hand on Don Bosco's arm....

"Will you let me come to the Oratory?"

"You want to be one of Don Bosco's boys?"

"Yes, Father."

"Then, come to the Oratory, because to tell the honest truth, I see a lot of good material in you."

"Oh?" asked Dominic. "Material that's good for what?"

"Good to become a saint!"

"A saint?... What kind of material can make a saint?"

"You'll find out. I'll show you—you'll be the cloth and I'll be the tailor. If you give me your complete trust, I'll mold you into a priceless garment for God. From this moment on, I consider you as one of Don Bosco's boys. Now go into the next room for a few minutes while I talk to your father."

Only then did the priest and the boy notice Charles Savio. The big blacksmith had tears in his eyes. After all, he was the only loser. He and his wife were giving up their oldest son, and even though his family would continue to grow, no one could take Dominic's place. The boy left the room....

"Now, Mr. Savio, how soon can he come?"

* * * * * * *

October 29, 1854, was set for Dominic's departure day. Mama Bridget had been sniffling around the house for days and Papa was strangely quiet. You couldn't hear his big voice booming in laughter, and his supper conversation no longer consisted of the humorous incidents of the day or tales of when he was young.

The departure day arrived. Dominic kissed Mama and his sister, Raimonda. It wasn't as if he were going forever, of course! There were whole summers and even special occasions when the boy would return to his home in Mondonio. He had to grow up and leave home sooner or later, Mama Bridget convinced herself. But, he was the first and still so young.

"Come on, son! We'd better leave now if we want to catch that coach. If we miss it,...it will be a mighty long walk to Turin."

Mr. Savio and Dominic made the stagecoach trip to Turin. Papa Savio knocked on the door of Don Bosco's Oratory. A small, older woman answered. Her face was kind and motherly. She looked down at the boy and asked:

"Who might you be?"

"I am Dominic Savio, and I have come here to live with Don Bosco."

"Oh, of course! My son said to expect you! And this must be your father. Welcome, Mr. Savio, to Don Bosco's Oratory. I will give you some refreshments and call my son."

When Don Bosco walked into a room his presence filled it. His magnetic personality dwarfed anyone else. He believed in the goodness of all people, at least in their good will if their actions contradicted the right. He never made anyone feel inferior or bad. He looked for the best side of each person, found it, and then built his friendship upon that! This ordinary peasant priest felt at home with princes or scrub ladies, bishops or hoodlums. And he left an unforgettable impression upon each one.

Dominic's anxieties faded away in the presence of Don Bosco. He felt secure...ready...to begin his new life there. He looked up at his father; his eyes shone with joy.

"I'm at home here, Dad!"

"I know...I leave contented, knowing that my boy is in the best of hands. Anything that you need, Don Bosco, or anything that I can do for you, just write, or tell my son to. Can this old smithy have your blessing?"

The boy and his father knelt down as the priest pronounced the words and blessed them.

The priest and Dominic were alone now. There was silence; the boy needed a few minutes of recuperation after his father's departure. Then Dominic turned his attention to Don Bosco.

"You promised you would show me how to become a *saint*.... It must be awfully hard to be a saint!"

"Why do you say that?"

"Because so few people live that way!"

"That doesn't mean it's hard. They need to be shown the way to become saints!"

"But don't saints happen only once in a great while?"

"No! All people are called to be saints. Jesus said: 'You are to be perfect even as your heavenly Father is perfect.' That is why you too, son, must try with all your might to become a saint!"

"Me?"

"Of course!"

"But what is a saint—a statue with a halo and lily?"

"No, not that easy! A saint is a person who lives his whole life trying to please God in the best way possible, doing His will cheerfully, continuously."

"Oh...I never knew saints were like that—I mean plain, ordinary people who are trying their best to be very good.... You mean...then I,...even I can become a saint?"

"Yes."

The priest smiled. The boy put his small hand inside Don Bosco's large hand.

"Will you show me how?"

"With the help of God, that is just what I will do, son. That is just what I will do!"

Life for Dominic at Don Bosco's Oratory was full of joy and new experiences. There was so much to learn, especially about God, and the way of life that leads to God. Don Bosco was always ready to answer questions, to talk things over, to lead by example. Many times he would repeat:

"Think of yourselves as the cloth, boys, and think of me as the tailor."

Don Bosco, God's tailor, was, by his work for boys, weaving many wonderful garments for God. He was an optimistic builder on the best of all that was human to lead his youth to the eternal.

But while all was going so well, God's will for Dominic Savio was to take another course. By February of 1857, he was very ill. The knife-like pains that ripped his stomach were searing his forehead, too.

"You called me, Don Bosco?"

"You know, Dominic, I'm going to try your faith a little. I want you to go home to Mondonio to get well. With your mother's home cooking and all that care, not to mention the peace and quiet of your little town—I think *that* is just what you need to get back on your feet again."

"But...you didn't finish your job!"

"Job?"

"Yes, you are the tailor and you promised to make me a saint."

"I haven't abandoned the task. This, too, is another thread in your cloak of sanctity, because God is asking a great sacrifice of you. Trust me in this, Dominic, as you have trusted me in all else since the first day we met. Your father will come tomorrow. He will take you home to get well.... Continue at home to practice all that you learned here, son. I will write to you and direct you. That is the least that a *good* tailor would do. Hurry back, strong and well, and go on to your priestly goal."

The goodbyes at the Oratory were painful. The boys all clustered around their friend.

"Bye, Dom, hurry back."

"We're with you all the way!"

"You'll be back before we even have time to miss you."

But Dominic's eyes had a far-away look as he said:

"I won't come back to the Oratory, like this anyway,...but, I'll be with you from heaven."

Mr. Savio picked up the bundles and waited patiently for his son. Dominic turned around, glanced at Don Bosco and the boys and waved, wearing a remarkable smile. That was the last picture, the last remembrance the boys at the Oratory had of Dominic Savio—always happy, in victory, in defeat, always a winner because he was big enough to accept God's will in every circumstance of his life.

The rest of the story is history. Young Dominic Savio went back to Mondonio and followed in simplicity and joy, the path made clear by his beloved Don Bosco. And even though death was to claim him while still a teenager, he had, with God's help, attained the greatest goal of all—sanctity.

A few months passed by. A letter was placed on Don Bosco's desk. It was a brief note penned in the large, careful handwriting of Charles Savio, which read:

"My son, my little boy, is dead."

Don Bosco whispered as he prayed alone in chapel, "You were right, Dominic. You didn't return to the Oratory. But while you were right about that, you were wrong about something else. From heaven, at last you can see that I didn't leave my job as tailor undone. You see, son, the garment was ready for God."

11

how
much
should
I
give
my
God?

The eighteenth century French climate was like a pressure cooker near the exploding point. Not exactly the proper atmosphere for the birth of a saint! No sooner had John Vianney been born, than the French Revolution began. His parents, Matthew and Marie Vianney were peasants from a country town called Dardilly.

"Mama, let's be ready before the sun goes down. Mass will be at Old Ben's in the village."

"Good, closer this time. We won't have to travel as far. You have the cart ready outside the door, Papa, and I'll bundle up the children."

"Marie,...I wonder if being a Catholic will ever get easier here in France?"

Mrs. Vianney laughed at her husband's remark and then her face grew serious as she said:

"You know, if you think about it, being a good Catholic can never really be easy. After all, Jesus' life was full of sacrifice and if we're His followers, we don't want to have things *too* easy."

Matthew Vianney smiled. He kissed his wife on the forehead and said softly: "That's why I married you...because you make good sense!"

Matthew and Marie carted the children with them into dark dungeons or wherever else Mass was being said. They were fools, you might say. But life was not a game of chance with them—it was a matter of faith!

Time passed, and their eldest son John, an unusually tall, lanky lad, presented himself to Father Balley at the Presbytery school nearby. The kindly, middle-aged rector extended his hand in welcome.

"I am Father Balley."

"And...I am John Vianney.... I want to become a priest, you know!"

"Yes, that is what your pastor has told me."

He patted the shy young man on the shoulder and added, "I want you to become a priest, too."

And so, John Vianney launched his great quest for the priesthood. The work was hard, slow...and progress was equally hard and equally slow. To one who could barely read or write, to take on the study of Latin required courage and faith...a lot more faith than John had. It was Father Balley's faith that saw him through the first painful year of seminary preparation. John was discouraged.

"I should quit!"

Father Balley laughed and chided, "Over a little bit of Latin? Oh, no...you won't give up that easily."

John resumed his studies. Time passed and brought with it some major and minor setbacks, but the boy still clung fast to his priestly goal. He went home to Dardilly to see his dying mother.

"John, I want you to be a priest so much. I want to see you a priest."

John stroked her forehead and she smiled.

"Mother, you look as if your prayer is already answered, as though you *know* I will be a priest."

"Faith, son, oh how we need faith!"

"You have faith, don't you, Mother?" Téars danced in his eyes as he pleaded, "Then, have faith that I can learn that impossible Latin!"

She grasped his hand and smiled. Death came to her quietly, almost gently. At last her earthly bonds were broken, and she was free, wonderfully free, to do her work from heaven.

John went to live with the holy pastor of Ecully, Father Balley. The priest was jubilant and so was John. Father Balley sent John to the minor seminary at Verrieres, and then to the major seminary at Lyons. The major seminary was much more difficult. In fact, all the classes were conducted in Latin. John tried his best...but after six months, the rector invited him to his office.

"Sit down, John. Let's talk about you."

"About me, Father?"

The priest noticed the tenseness in John's face and his voice rang with kindness.

"Yes, you. You see, John, I want to do what I feel is best for you. I know how badly you want to be a priest. And you'll never know how much it costs me to...advise you otherwise, but you see, son, the studies required are far beyond your grasp. Go home, in peace, and serve God as best you can in the way that He chooses."

For John, home was now Ecully; he went back to Father Balley. A lonely lad with hands in pockets, he presented himself at the good priest's doorstep. He sat down, and in halting phrases, confused and bewildered, he told the story of failure and discouragement. He said flatly, "I've decided...to become a brother!"

"You will become what God *wants* you to become, John. And I believe with all my heart that God wants you to become a priest!"

John became the object of Father Balley's private coaching, and then he was questioned by a group of priest examiners. Panic raced through his body. He knew the answers, but he only stammered and repeated useless phrases. It was not much of an impression that he made. And he did not pass the examination.

"All right, Father Balley, now you have to admit that God doesn't want me to be a priest."

The priest looked up at him with a questioning glance.

"Why, no, son. The thought never even occurred to me."

Father Balley was like a rubber punching bag—the harder the punch, the more he bounced right back into action. John continued studying with greater intensity. When Father Balley felt that the young man was ready, he took the slowest seminarian in all of France to see the bishop.

Bishop Courbon looked at the tall, eager young man before him. He thought of all the parishes left vacant by the French Revolution, and then looked back at John again. Turning to Father Balley, he asked, "Is John Vianney good?"

"He is a model of goodness."

"Very well, then, let him be ordained. The grace of God will do the rest."

John Vianney was ordained a priest on August 13, 1815. Then it was back to Ecully...back to Father Balley. The whole town was waiting for the young man who had long ago stolen their hearts.

"Father John! Father John!"

They kissed his consecrated hands. He was their boy, the object of so many prayers, and they shared in the joy of the victory as well. John tried to pull away as fast as he could. There was someone else he had to see. John knocked nervously on the rectory door. The door quickly opened. Two priests stood looking at each other. Finally Father Balley managed to say:

"Come in, son, come in. See, what did I tell you? Ah, my friend, I never doubted the will of God in your regard. He chose you to be His priest. And I said to myself: 'A priest he will be!' "

John became Father Balley's curate. Three years passed by, the happiest years of Father John's young life. And then, the saintly Father Balley became very sick and lay dying. Still his thoughts were on his curate more than on himself.

"My life on this earth is over, John. But, you know, it's really the beginning.... Just think, heaven will never end. And. I will still be with you...from that blessed place. You struggled to become a priest, my son! I tell you in the name of God...all your life you will bless that struggle which will make you more sensitive to the needs of thousands of people hungering for God's peace. And you alone, my Vianney, will bring them that peace through the sacrament of Penance."

Father John buried his friend's body in a plain little graveyard in that country town of Ecully. But the spirit of Father Balley followed his beloved Vianney to his next assignment. Grateful memories flooded John's mind of a man, a good man, and a great priest, whom he could never forget. His thoughts were of Father Balley as he trekked the road to Ars.

Someone described the little town of Ars, France, as "in every sense of the word, a hole." The words of the bishop rang in Father John's ears: "My friend, you have been appointed Curé of Ars. It is a little parish where there is not much love of God; you must put some into it."

"Yes, that is what I must do...bring these poor people the love of their God."

Father Vianney had big plans for Ars. He preached, taught catechism classes, visited each family and doubled the physical penances he had begun as a curate to Father

Balley. Spiritual victories, more than the Curé dared hope for, were pouring into his lap. But he suffered plenty for them. Half-starved, praying for hours, physical penances, wasn't this enough to pay for the conversion of a town? Evidently not, because even the devil came to plague his private moments. From 1824 to 1858, hell followed Vianney in the most harsh and extreme of ways...but the devil never won.

It was too good to be true...the life of this remarkable man, that is. Ars could not hide him for themselves. Pilgrims brought more pilgrims. The Curé asked a penitent, "But, my friend, why did you come from such a great distance to Ars?"

Through muffled sobs, the man stumbled his reply, "Father, I settled on hell a long time ago. And I made up my mind that my sins were too rotten to tell anybody.... Then some people passed through my town. They said that there was a priest that could straighten out anybody's life. And I made up my mind to *find you* if I had to walk the length of France!"

The Curé spent sixteen to seventeen hours a day in the confessional. A few sought him out of curiosity and returned from necessity. Some tried to hide the state of their soul or to conceal a sin and he would tell them what was missing. Sometimes he would weep at the tale of offenses against God, and after each sin would say, "What a pity! What a pity!"

The prayers of Father Vianney followed each person as he or she left the church and walked out into the light of ordinary living. He never forgot a single person.

Father Vianney was determined."I've made up my mind! I will die working; yes, I will die working!"

"Hear my confession!"

"And mine..."

"Bless my children...."

"Pray for me!"

The Curé smiled and carefully fulfilled each request. But his life of dedication, of total giving, had demanded its toll on his health. He said with a smile, "I can do no more. Sinners will kill the sinner."

Over 100,000 pilgrims had come to Ars in that year of 1859. They came to find a man who resembled Christ as much as any human being could! And they were not disappointed. Now he lay dying.... His memory painted the picture of his forty-five years of priestly dedication; faces and events danced through the archives of his mind. He saw his family,...Bishop Courbon, and... especially the man who had been more responsible than any other human being for his priestly vocation—Father Balley. The Curé of Ars lingered on that sacred memory of the priest whose backbone had seen him through those early years. And his heart flooded with gratitude.

He made his confession, his last confession, and then a group of priests, each bearing a lighted candle, filed in solemn procession to his room. They brought with them the most beautiful gift that Father Vianney could ask for. Now that he could no longer come to the Master, the Master had come to him. He whispered softly, "It's sad to be making one's last Communion...."

And then he died, silently...serenely. There was "no struggle, no violence, no agony." He just went to sleep on that sultry night in early August and awoke in eternity.

12

"someday,
I know,
he
will
change"

A familiar figure walked quickly down a narrow street in the small Italian village of Lovere. Two neighbor women shook their heads as they watched her pass. "There she goes again tonight," one remarked. "Our good neighbor, Modesto, must be drinking again. And there his daughter goes to bring him home."

"And to think," her friend added, "she was doing so well away at school. Modesto doesn't know what a good daughter he has. What a shame!"

Bartholomea Capitanio slipped quietly into the smoke-filled tavern. The smell of liquor and cigars and the coarse sound of drunken laughter was nothing new to her. Wishing she could run away, she forced herself on through the noisy clusters of men. A hush filled the tavern as this determined young woman drew close to her father.

"Papa," she coaxed, as she placed her hand in his, "please come home now. Camilla and Mamma are waiting for you."

Modesto Capitanio, who was known in the taverns of Lovere for his hot temper and gambling talents, silently followed his strong-willed daughter into the sobering air of evening. Only Bartholomea's firm yet gentle character could calm her father during his violent outbursts. Modesto preferred this daughter of his in a special way because of the respect she always showed to him.

As they walked home, Bartholomea silently prayed, "My Jesus, please help my father to be kind to Mamma tonight. He doesn't know what he is doing when he's drunk. O my God, help him!" Memories of nights spent consoling her mother flashed through her mind. Often when her father came home drunk he was ready to fight with his wife, Catherine, over the smallest matter. As Bartholomea helped to steady her father's clumsy walk, she recalled the times he had driven her good mother from their home and worse still the times he had beaten her. "But he is my father," she reflected. "Someday, I *know*, he will change."

It had been hard for Bartholomea Capitanio to return to her home town of Lovere in July, 1824. How much she had loved the boarding school conducted by the Sisters of St. Clare, where she had spent most of her happy teen years!

In her last months there she had even been chosen to help teach the younger children. Bartholomea had loved that. She had striven to be patient, understanding, lively and always able to face any situation—the way a teacher *should* be. By correcting the children when they needed it and encouraging them in difficulties, she had tried to be not only a teacher but their friend.

Looking back on those happy days, Bartholomea could clearly remember the way she had gathered the children around her after recreation to teach them new prayers or tell the stories of the saints which were always a favorite! Those were happy years for Bartholomea —years she would always remember.

But then her parents had asked her to leave school and return home. "It is God's will," she had said, but how hard it had been for her to leave the good sisters and the children. Deep within herself she had felt a stirring to stay on at school, not only to be a teacher but also to become a sister herself.

Looking back on those happy days, Bartholomea could clearly remember the way she had gathered the children around her after recreation to teach them new prayers or tell the stories of the saints which were always a favorite! Those were happy years for Bartholomea—years she would always remember.

Bartholomea had prepared herself for her new life at home by praying, "O Lord, help me to be understanding with my father. Help me never to be ashamed of him. Give me the strength to swallow my pride and to love him as You love him."

And now Bartholomea felt that she was indeed receiving the strength she had asked for. True, her natural pride flared up each time she stepped into a bar to bring her father home. The smell, the laughter and the looks she received all made her sick, but she wouldn't run. "He is my father," she would repeat over and over, and the Lord would come to her aid.

One night Bartholomea arrived on the scene as a neighbor was insulting her father. Modesto's fierce temper welled up within him and he lunged at the other man.

"Papa," called Bartholomea, running up to him. "It's not worth bothering about. It's not worth it. Come on, let's go home."

Somehow that determined voice and small, strong hand got through to the angry man. Father and daughter turned away from the tormentor and left the tavern together.

Shortly after her return home, Bartholomea earned a teacher's diploma and opened a school for little girls in her parents' house. Beyond the usual classroom subjects, Bartholomea stressed kindness, patience and respect for one another.

The young teacher herself gave a great example of patience. Her pupils could see this. But little could the children know of the virtue Bartholomea exercised within her own family—especially with Camilla.

Camilla was her sister—five years her junior, fiery and impatient. The younger girl ordered the elder about continually. And Bartholomea always hastened to obey, even though some days her patience was really tested.

With her energetic and enterprising character, how did Bartholomea manage to give in to her sister continually? Through a well-planned spiritual program. In fact, one of the points in this program was this: "I shall be pleasant and kind to everyone, especially to my sister."

That program of life reveals much about Bartholomea's swift growth in holiness. For example, she wrote:

"I shall never complain about anything or tell others about the little sufferings which God may send me.

"I shall try to hide my likes and dislikes, following instead the preferences of the others. I shall choose the simplest food and clothes, unless my companions wish otherwise.

"I shall hold my tongue, never saying unkind or useless words.

"I shall never pry into the affairs of others, but shall concentrate on my own.

"I shall never praise myself or give excuses, but shall try to remain hidden from the eyes of people in order to be more pleasing to God.

"I shall bear insults, sharp words, and other harshness patiently and joyously."

And—as is always true of those who have a great love of God and desire to be holy, Bartholomea also cultivated a great love for her neighbor. Her program reveals this fact in the following lines:

"I shall love the poor and enjoy being with them. I shall help them with kind words and with as much material aid as possible. Three times a week I shall put aside some of my own food to give to them.

"I shall visit the sick as often as I can—at least once a week.

"On every holy day I shall give some religious instruction to someone who needs it.

"I shall teach classes only to give glory to God and help my neighbor.

"I shall never refuse to do someone a favor, no matter how inconvenient it may be.

"I shall never argue or raise my voice. On the contrary, I shall try to keep peace in my family."

Who inspired Bartholomea Capitanio to draw up and follow such a demanding program of Christian heroism? Perhaps we find the answer in another excerpt from her writings:

"I shall have great trust in my sweet Mother Mary and shall turn to her in every need. When tempted, I shall call upon her. Through her help I am confident of reaching heaven."

Bartholomea Capitanio was a born teacher. Her pupils learned quickly, and much more than reading, writing and arithmetic! After a few months, parents were amazed at what lambs their unruly youngsters had become.

The young woman's teaching method was this—to love her pupils and sacrifice herself for them. Seeing how truly she loved them, the children responded with all their best efforts. Every day Bartholomea would propose a virtue for them to practice. Often she rewarded those who did best.

She helped each child, never showing partiality. She did not hesitate to point out faults, but in such a kind way that the pupil would try at once for self-improvement.

Pastors of parishes in nearby towns began to send teenage girls to Bartholomea, so that they would learn to teach as she did. In that way the young woman's influence spread throughout the whole district, which comprised over eighty villages!

In 1826, with Catherine Gerosa, another good woman of her district, Bartholomea opened a hospital to care for the poor. Often her small figure would be seen visiting from bed to bed encouraging and helping the patients with their spiritual needs as well as the physical.

One man, who was more sick in spirit than in health, ignored Bartholomea's urgings to make a good confession. But in time and with much prayer, he returned to the sacraments and friendship with God. After leaving the hospital, this contrite man became a brother. Whenever he heard anyone speak of Lovere, he would say, "There is a saint in that town!"

In the fall of 1831, Modesto Capitanio was dying. Always concerned for her father's welfare, his elder daughter nursed and prayed for him.

"Papa," she would plead, "tell Jesus you are sorry. Ask Him to forgive, and to give you the strength to make a good confession."

After a long struggle with himself, Modesto *did* make a good confession. He confided to the priest that it was his daughter who had led him to do it.

After her father's peaceful death, Bartholomea wept, but she knew he had died sorry for his sins and secure in God's mercy.

At this time Bartholomea and Catherine Gerosa were totally absorbed in their expanding apostolate— tending the sick, helping to find homes for abandoned children, and taking care of the elderly. Seeing the need for a new religious congregation, the two founded a community of sisters dedicated to works of charity.

The Institute of the Sisters of Charity of Lovere came into being on the Feast of the Presentation of Mary in 1832. But as the congregation was just beginning, Bartholomea's life was rapidly ending: she had contracted tuberculosis. Dying now meant leaving the institute in other hands. But the young foundress trusted in God's Divine Providence, which guides and directs all things. Willingly she offered her life for the good of the new congregation.

To comfort her mother and the faithful of her village who stayed with her during her last illness, Bartholomea would often say: "This is the moment when God in His mercy will receive me into paradise. Don't be saddened by my death, but instead thank God!"

On July 26, 1833, Bartholomea clasped a crucifix and a small statue of the Blessed Mother for the last time. "My Jesus, how good You are to me! I love You. Holy Mother of God, pray for us sinners now and at the hour of our death." A short time after, at the age of twenty-six, Bartholomea died.

For a time it seemed as if the foundation would crumble into nothingness. Catherine Gerosa, less enterprising than Bartholomea and almost alone, became very discouraged. Only the urging of a holy priest finally persuaded her to go ahead without the leadership of her departed companion.

Camilla Capitanio and some of Bartholomea's former pupils soon joined Catherine Gerosa. About two years after Bartholomea's death, the members of this little group received the religious habit.

And then the congregation began to grow. It spread throughout Italy and sent missionaries to India and Brazil. A hundred years after its foundation the Sisters of Charity of Lovere numbered 8,150 sisters helping 240,000 people daily—abandoned children, the elderly, lepers, the mentally ill, teenagers who had gone astray....

On May 22, 1950, over a hundred years after Bartholomea's death, both she and Catherine Gerosa were proclaimed saints by Pope Pius XII in St. Peter's packed Basilica.

Perhaps it was Bartholomea's conviction—"Someday my father will change!"—and because she did something about it, that her life of charity and holiness began. It may have seemed a small thing—Bartholomea's loving concern for her father, but because she loved her father in God, this love helped give rise to great sanctity in her soul and a new religious congregation in the Church.

13

to keep a promise

Clouds of dust choked the Santa Fe Trail as the coach rumbled along. Sharp eyes scanned the horizon and strong hands nervously fingered cocked revolvers. For weeks now not a single stagecoach or buggy had been free from the terrorizing attacks of outlaws. And now a scout had just returned with the breathless message that a horseman was heading straight this way—and coming fast.

Suddenly a black-bonneted head poked out of the coach window. "If the comer is a scout for the gang, I think our best bet is to play passive. I'd suggest putting revolvers out of sight, gentlemen."

The men looked at the twenty-seven-year-old nun as if she had completely lost her mind. Obviously this naïve creature had no idea at all of how to handle desperadoes.

"Please put your revolvers away." Her voice wasn't begging, nor was it aggressive. She was so convincingly unafraid it was almost irritating. One by one the weapons slid out of view.

Within seconds, furious hoof-beats broke the stillness as the bandit descended on the lone coach. Brandishing his six-shooter, he galloped alongside and peered in. Sister Blandina shifted her bonnet and peered right back.

Their eyes met. Then the outlaw respectfully raised his broad-brimmed hat, waved, bowed, and disappeared. It was Billy the Kid.

Stupefied, the other passengers and the drivers exchanged unbelieving glances. Sister Blandina returned to the business of traveling as if nothing had happened, and nobody had the courage to ask her what had. It wasn't a sudden streak of chivalry on the part of a murderer. Only a small band of outlaws and a smaller band of nuns knew the reason: Billy the Kid was merely keeping a promise.

Not quite a year before, Sister Blandina had trekked day after day to an out-of-the-way adobe hut, carrying a basket of food, linens and medicines. Her business was saving bodies as well as souls. And this time the body and soul in question belonged to a wounded member of Billy the Kid's gang. When all four of the town's doctors had refused to treat the injured man, Sister Blandina had taken it upon herself.

Her efforts at moral recovery left no apparent results. But her nursing did. The man recovered, and a grateful Billy the Kid came personally to thank her. When he, in Herodian fashion, promised her any favor she would ask, she took him up on it immediately.

"Yes, there is a favor you can grant me."

"The favor's granted," he said, extending his hand.

The intrepid Sister of Charity and the murderer, who looked all the innocence of a small boy, shook hands. Then she matter-of-factly told him she'd like him to cancel the real reason he'd come—to scalp the four town doctors, among whom was the convent physician!

"She's game," whispered her ex-patient.

The Kid spoke. "I granted you the favor before I knew what it was, and it stands.... And, Sister, any time my pals and I can serve you, we're ready."

So travelers on the Santa Fe trail were guaranteed safe passage in Sister Blandina's company. Yet there was nothing triumphalistic about her. When a sheriff's bullet ended the young outlaw's murderous career, she wept as if for a son. And she prayed. In a letter she wrote sorrowfully:

"He started on the downhill road at the age of twelve. Somebody had insulted his mother, and he took revenge. Poor, poor boy! If only we had reached him *then*, before so many murders...."

In Christianity's infancy a young virgin named Blandina astounded her persecutors with her obstinate courage and joyful heroism. Threats, promises, tortures—every attempt to sway the seemingly delicate creature was like ramming against an iron wall.

Almost eighteen centuries later a dark-eyed Italian emigrant knelt in a Cincinnati convent chapel and received the black bonnet of the Sisters of Charity. With the bonnet came the new name—Blandina. The similarity proved to be more than coincidental.

Homesteaders, politicians, gold-miners, outlaws, epidemics, Indian raids.... Yes, convent life was far from dull in the days of America's Wild West. And dullness and Sister Blandina seem never to have been even passing acquaintances.

It was a normal day in 1874—as normal a day as could be had, that is, in young Colorado. Sister Blandina glanced up from her lesson preparations as a tall, sheepish-looking boy entered the classroom.

"S'str, can my sister...can she not come to school...?"

The nun's dark eyes met the boy's. He looked like a ghost. She avoided the question, and asked her own, "John, what happened?"

"Haven't you heard, Sister?"

"Nothing that should make you look as you do!"

"Sister, Dad shot a man. He's in jail. There's a mob and men 'bout forty feet from the jail by Mr. McCaferty's room—that's the man got shot, Sister. Soon as he dies, they're going to signal and then the mob'll go to the jail and drag Dad out...and hang him."

Sister Blandina listened in horror. She had seen mob law at work before. It *must not* be allowed to work on John's father.

"Haven't you thought of anything that might save your father?"

"Nothing, Sister. There's nothing can be done," the boy said in desolation.

"But isn't there any hope the man—Mr. McCaferty— might recover?"

"No way, Sister. He might last a day or so, but no more'n that. The gun was loaded with tin shot."

The boy looked down at Sister Blandina's bowed bonnet. Was she praying or thinking, he wondered. Must be both, thought John. It seemed like Sister Blandina always did both at the same time, though he never could figure out how. Suddenly she raised her head and jolted the boy back to reality.

"John, go to jail and ask your father if he'll take a chance at not being hanged by a mob."

"What are you going to do, Sister?"

"First, we'll visit the wounded man and ask if he'll see and forgive your father." She paused, then added softly, "...with the understanding that the real law will be carried out."

"Sister, that mob will tear him to pieces before he's ten feet from the jail!"

The nun looked straight at the boy. She was firm. "And I believe they *won't*—not if a Sister goes with him. That's the only thing I can see that will save him from the mob, John. Ask your father to decide. We'll visit the sick man as soon as school's out today."

The setting sun was just touching the dusty town with its gold when Sister Blandina and her companion left the wounded Mr. McCaferty's room. She had won his promise of forgiveness for John's father. Later that night, a breathless John came with his report. His father was afraid to do it, but if Sister would go with him, he'd risk it.

The next day dawned hot and heavy. And Sister Blandina felt more than the heat hanging in the Colorado air as she entered the sheriff's office. He greeted her pleasantly.

"Good morning, Mr. Sheriff. Needless to ask if you know what's taking place out there...."

"You mean the lynch mob waiting for the prisoner?"

"Exactly. What are you going to do to prevent the lynching?"

The six-foot-four sheriff stood open-mouthed before the five-foot-three nun. He couldn't believe her question.

"*Do?* Do! What has any sheriff here ever been able to *do* to stop a *mob?*"

The woman in black looked up at him with a calm that unnerved him.

"Be the first sheriff to make the attempt!" she said evenly.

"How, Sister? How?" he moaned.

She told him the plan: the prisoner would walk between the sheriff and herself to the wounded man's room to ask forgiveness. That would enable an official trial and the real law to take charge.

"Sister, have you ever seen the workings of a mob?" the sheriff interrupted.

"A few, Mr. Sheriff."

"And you'd take the chance of having the prisoner dragged from between the both of us and hanged on the nearest cottonwood?" He shook his head in disbelief.

With her usual poise, the nun was undaunted. "In my opinion, there is nothing to fear."

For a moment, the silence was deafening. Then, disarmed, the sheriff shrugged his shoulders.

"Well, if you're not afraid...neither am I."

The fiery sun beat down from mid-sky as the three figures walked down the middle of Trinidad's dusty main street: the sheriff, the prisoner, the nun. Conversations melted into silence as the trio passed the groups of men evenly spaced along the street that led to the room where young Mr. McCaferty lay dying. The crowd was tense and seemed to be counting every creak of the men's leather boots, every jingle of the rosary at the nun's side.

When they reached their destination, another cluster of tough westerners blocked the door to the room where the young Irishman lay. Hatred flashed in their eyes. "Revenge," noted Sister Blandina. Fear clutched at her. Would they grab their man just as they got to the door? Would John see his father hanged right before his eyes? "Oh, God," she prayed quietly, "help us...."

Slowly, silently, the crowd made way. The prisoner stood on the threshold. "Go in," Sister Blandina urged softly.

Inside the room, the prisoner looked at the man he had shot. He's just a little older than my John, the prisoner mused. Then he stammered, "I...I'm sorry. I didn't know what I was doing. I'm sorry, boy. Forgive me...."

From his deathbed the young Irishman said slowly, "I forgive you, as I hope to be forgiven...but the law must take its course."

At the door, Sister Blandina repeated the conversation aloud to the waiting mob. "Yes, *the law* must take its course—*not mob law!*"

One by one, the members of the lynch mob dispersed. The clusters of hate-filled men broke up along the street and made their way to horses or homes, leaving dust in the torrid air of Trinidad, and leaving justice to the law.

Sister Blandina didn't see them go. Her eyes were wet with tears, and closed in a heartfelt, grateful prayer.

When Sister Blandina set out to do a thing, it got done. More than once she single-handedly averted an Indian attack that could have wiped out an entire town. The Indians trusted her. They listened to her. This woman always kept her word. And because of her, they would keep theirs.

The little nun who could devoutly pray her rosary one minute and deftly carve a bullet out of a man's chest the next, understandably became a frontier heroine. And *became* is the key word. For it wasn't fame, or money, or adventure that sent Sister Blandina Segale across the prairies with wagon trains and stagecoaches. It was love of God and His people. Love of immortal souls that were all too easily being lost while the West was being won. Love that was a process of "becoming" through sweat and toil, hardship and prayer. The little girl who once used to sit on her father's fruit cart, who had loved flowers and pretty clothes, had to learn to love the dust and grime, the smells and sights of the untamed West, because these were part and parcel of the people she served. Work meant not only teaching and nursing or going on endless errands of mercy, but the self-conquest that had to be at their base.

"Do whatever presents itself, and never omit anything because of hardship or repugnance."

That was the motto Sister Blandina had chosen for herself on her first mission assignment. And when God called her home at the age of ninety-one, men of every race and creed rose up to praise the quiet, black-bonneted woman who had kept her resolve.

Perhaps that was what men admired most in Sister Blandina Segale. Certainly it was what God did....

14

no
pennies
for
Pauline

Paris, June, 1849. Mademoiselle Pauline Jaricot stood rigid, in front of the President of the Propagation of the Faith. He held Pauline's credentials in his hands. Calmly Pauline explained her visit. "Mr. President, as the Foundress of the Propagation of the Faith, I'm here to ask a big favor. The model Christian town we started two years ago is badly in need of finances. But I'm sure with a few pennies from each member of the Propagation of the Faith we can easily pay our debt. Then, at least in one small town in France, the working classes will be able to lead decent Christian lives."

The President's eyes opened wide in disbelief. "Did I hear you correctly, Mademoiselle? Did you say that *you* are the *Foundress* of the Propagation of the Faith?"

"Yes, Monsieur. I was twenty at the time. But I am not here to gain recognition—only help."

The President glanced down again at the credentials. "I'm afraid you are mistaken, Mademoiselle. Our Society was founded by a poor, obscure servant girl whose name has long been forgotten."

"What?" Pauline stammered.

"Yes, Mademoiselle. We have evidence here in our files which proves this."

With that he handed Pauline a folder containing the article.

With trembling hand the dignified heiress read the account.

"Why, this is absurd!" she exclaimed. "I am the Society's foundress and no one else! It's true that the work passed into the hands of someone else, but the original idea and organization were my own. Please, in the name of justice, give me the help that I now ask!"

Coldly the President answered, "I'm sorry; I can do nothing. I must first consult the members of my council. Come back in a week's time."

Pauline could hardly believe it, and after a week's time she heard the verdict—no help would be forthcoming. The members of the council didn't voice their opinion but it was implied: Mademoiselle Jaricot was a scheming, ambitious woman who wanted to be made a lot of in her old age. Wasn't she satisfied with all the pomp and honor connected with her being the foundress of the Living Rosary and the Association of the Holy Childhood? All those trips to Rome and worldwide recognition had really turned her head. Now she wanted to take the credit for starting the world famous Propagation of the Faith too?

Pauline was numb with shock and disappointment. Then she did what had been so repugnant to her. She went out to beg from door to door accompanied by her faithful Maria Dubouis.

It was very hard to begin to beg at the age of fifty. In former years, Pauline Jaricot, a millionaire's daughter, had had free access to her father's money, and after his death she had received her own substantial share of the estate. Now, together with the meager funds she was able to collect, came abundant abuse and insult.

But Pauline stayed on in Paris for fifteen months. In the meantime she sent appeals for help to Lyons, her hometown. She had many friends there in the Propagation of the Faith. For sure, they would help her.

Another shock almost crushed her completely. Lyons not only refused financial help, but they would also oppose any of her efforts to collect funds elsewhere. Why, the enormous debt was of her own doing. Let her pay for it herself.

"Lord, it's too much," Pauline groaned. "Really, I can't bear any more."

But more she did bear. When she returned home, she found that many of her friends had left her and now even her own family refused to supply any more funds for her works of charity. Pauline was forced to sell the model town and the property at a tremendous loss and to apply for relief from the parish. On February 26, 1853, Mademoiselle Pauline Jaricot claimed extreme need for herself and the four women living with her, and with the pastor's signature on the certificate, the Jaricot household began to receive public charity for food, clothes and fuel. Deeply hurt, Pauline presented the certificate to her Daughters of Mary. With a brave smile she announced lightly, "See, here's my title of nobility!"

At the age of sixteen Pauline Jaricot, the charming daughter of a prosperous silk merchant, had been very much preoccupied with parties, her appearance, and with favorable comments of the members of high society.

But, after an accident and a long, painful illness, and hearing a sermon on vanity, the lively young socialite suddenly changed. The change was so drastic that everyone who knew Pauline thought the poor girl had lost her mind.

One Sunday, Pauline put away her fashionable gowns, her glittering jewels and her elegant shoes. She donned a drab, ugly purple dress, wore the coarse muslin cap of a working girl to hide her beautiful curls, and slipped her dainty feet into clumsy wooden sandals. Trembling with the supreme effort she was making, she then proceeded down the main aisle of church. All heads turned at the sound of the clattering sandals. At each audible gasp, Pauline's cheeks burned hotter. She stumbled into the pew and wished she could have disappeared. She was sick with shame. What were people thinking of her? And what a humiliation for the family too! And yet, if she was to break with her old life, half-way measures would never do!

She had offered this sacrifice to God to obtain the grace of knowing what He wanted her to do. She felt God wanted something of her, yet she was afraid of what it might be.

Gradually the Lord made His will known and Pauline began her works of charity and dedication to the sick in the hospitals and the workers in the factories.

When she was twenty, Pauline organized groups of the poor into tens, hundreds, and thousands with a leader for each group. The dues for each member were a penny a week. The small donations from all the faithful would be sent for the foreign missions in China.

The Society of the Propagation of the Faith, as the organized groups were called, grew rapidly and became famous. Then in May, 1822, some people who were annoyed that a mere woman—a mere girl at that—should have even thought of such an organization, succeeded in taking the organization from Pauline's hands. They gave it new direction and made it embrace, not only the missions of China, but all the missions in the world. Pauline, somewhat reluctantly, withdrew quietly into the background. She tried to stifle her feelings of resentment, and continued working for the success of the Society.

Continuing to live at home, Pauline took care of her aging father and also followed a strict routine of prayer and spiritual exercises in the cultivation of the interior life.

At the age of twenty-six, Mademoiselle Jaricot began a new apostolic institution: *The Living Rosary*. Five people recited a decade of the rosary each day and each person was to find five others and these five more and so on. Small annual dues would be collected from each member and used to pay for the distribution of good books, rosaries, statues and medals, to the poor. The association had two purposes—to make reparation for sinners and to promote the reading of religious books.

During its first year, over 150 groups had been established in France. And after only three years, the *Living Rosary* was founded in ten other countries including the United States and South America.

Pauline worked tirelessly to follow all the activities of the Propagation of the Faith and the Living Rosary. But the load of work proved too much and Pauline fell critically ill. After a miraculous cure and a pilgrimage of thanksgiving to Rome, in 1838, Pauline knelt at the feet of Pope Gregory XV and related her work in the Propagation of the Faith and the Living Rosary. "But it's not enough, Your Holiness," she told the Pope. "I want to do more for the working class."

"You'll think of something soon," he said. "I'm sure of that. I'll give you my blessing for the Living Rosary—for its growth and successful apostolate."

Then, in that year, she set forth to the Bishop of Nancy her plans for the Association of the Holy Childhood. Boys and girls could have their own missionary society.

Finally, in 1845, Pauline hit upon an idea for the working class. She would build a model town where Christian workers could live a decent Christian life. An ideal site was found in Rustrel and an enormous amount of money from individuals who believed in the cause was paid for the property.

However, the person in whom she had placed her trust for the financing of the project proved to be a fraud. After spending all the money on himself, he ended up in prison. But since he had acted in her name signing it to all transactions, Pauline was now the one responsible for the payment of the debt.

The hopes of receiving help from the Propagation of the Faith was the reason Mademoiselle Jaricot had gone to Paris in the summer of 1849.

Hundreds of people trusting in the name of Pauline Jaricot had placed their savings in her hands. Advised by her lawyers to declare bankruptcy, Pauline flashed back, "I'm not going to run away from my obligations. I know I've been a fool to be taken in by Gustave Perre. But every cent of this debt is going to be paid. And the interest on it too. Every cent, even if it takes the rest of my life!"

"All she wants is other people to pay her bills!"

"That's right. Pennies for Pauline!"

"Look at her blush, the wretch!"

"The fraud!"

Pauline bit her trembling lip in an effort to keep back her tears. This taunting and sneering was an almost everyday occurrence. As she came home from church, she whispered to Maria Dubuois, "It's...it's all right, my dear. All this is very good for my pride."

But in March, 1859, she herself felt she could bear no more. Braving a snowstorm and arriving half-frozen, sixty-year-old Pauline and her spiritual daughter, Maria, sat entranced in the bare, cold room of the Curé of Ars.

"My sisters," he addressed them, "to try to get from under the cross is to be crushed by its weight. But to suffer it with love and patience is to suffer no longer."

"Mon Pere," Pauline ventured, "but the debts: I want to pay them before I die."

"Perhaps this is your last and greatest cross. In heaven the good God will give you full justice and full understanding of why all this happened," soothed the Curé. Then he gave the venerable maiden a crucifix which bore the words, "God is my witness, Jesus is my model, Mary is my support. I ask nothing but love and sacrifice."

Pauline and Maria left consoled and strengthened. In a sermon the Curé of Ars testified, "I know one person who knows how to accept crosses, very heavy crosses, and who bears them with great love. It is Mademoiselle Jaricot of Lyons."

During her last days, this valiant daughter of the Church prayed for the salvation of all people and especially, for her beloved France. Pauline pressed her "certificate of nobility" close to her heart. For nine years it had proclaimed her utterly penniless. Looking up at her four loyal friends, Mademoiselle Jaricot exclaimed, "Suffering is *SO* important!" A few hours later, on January 9, 1862, after a fervent prayer to the Mother of God, the insolvent, sixty-two-year-old woman passed quietly to the mansions of heaven. She had carried her cross valiantly to the end.

The Society of the Propagation of the Faith continued to grow and flourish, as did the Living Rosary and the Association of the Holy Childhood. All were the fruit of one young woman's sacrifices and prayers and generosity in doing what God asked of her. May her prayer be ours, "Lord, give us saints. They alone renew and comfort the earth."

15

a poor
outcast

The Boston Common was ablaze with excitement! But the crowd which had gathered that night was quite different than the band of patriots who fought some hundred years before! Torches lit the darkness, flaring the tempers of the men who assembled there. Angry accusations filled the air as the crowd shouted in front of the bishop's residence:

"America for Americans!"

"No Catholics here!"

The crowd braved any possible insult and accusation.

Inside the small house, Bishop John Fitzpatrick collapsed in his chair with exhaustion. His chancellor, Father James Healy, stood near the door watching the mob's movement.

"Do you think they'll try to break in?" the bishop asked.

"No, I don't believe they'll go that far. For tonight I think they'll be satisfied to make noise."

The bishop looked up at the small, dark-skinned priest who shared his pastoral duties and worries. Bishop Fitzpatrick was filled with secret admiration for this young priest who had overcome so many difficulties.

Not many in Boston shared Bishop Fitzpatrick's esteem for this quiet priest; stories circulated about him like wildfire. Once Father Healy wrote to a friend: "The mercy of God has placed a poor outcast on a throne of glory that ill becomes him." "A poor outcast"—this was the theme of his life.

James Augustine Healy was born the son of an Irish plantation owner and his beautiful mulatto wife who had been born a slave. To James' father his wife's background had made no difference. He loved his wife and children and would protect them from any malicious tongues.

Numerous attempts to find a school that would accept James and his brothers were met with failure. But finally, by good fortune, two travelers met on a cargo ship in the spring of 1844—Bishop Fitzpatrick of Boston and Michael Healy, James' father.

"Mr. Healy, why don't you send your boys to Holy Cross College?" the bishop inquired when hearing of his problem. "There they will be accepted on ability alone. As long as your boys are willing to work hard, we don't care what the color of their skin is."

The following August, James and his three brothers sailed from Georgia to Massachusetts.

Young James Healy soon discovered that the color of his skin and the Irish brogue inherited from his father made no difference to his new classmates. Years passed, packed with hard study and fun. As graduation drew near, James decided his life's work—he would become a priest.

James longed to be a Jesuit. His fine intellect and highest class average indicated a vocation to the Society of Jesus. He loved Holy Cross College and hoped to return there as a teacher. However, his hopes were soon crushed. The Jesuit house of studies was located in Maryland and Maryland was a slave state. Legally a slave, James could be forced back to the South.

James was not to be disappointed for long. The Sulpicians in Montreal quickly accepted him. James Healy had graduated from college with the highest class average and a real spirit of determination; the color of his skin made no difference.

Long years of prayer and study followed both in Montreal and France. As the months flew by and ordination approached, James was racked with doubts: "Will they accept a black priest in America? Will they attend church when I celebrate Mass? Will they come to me to receive the sacraments?"

On June 10, 1854, Notre Dame was alive with majestic splendor. Its organ thundered throughout the cathedral as the ordination rite commenced. The Archbishop of Paris placed his hands on James' head: "You are a priest forever."

In August of that same year, Father Healy returned to Boston. His first assignment was as assistant to the House of the Guardian Angel, a home for more than a hundred boys. These boys, who had once roamed the Boston harbor area and back streets in search of food and shelter, had found a sure friend in Father Healy.

Besides his work at the Guardian Angel home, Father Healy soon became a familiar figure in the ghettoes. The steady flow of immigrants had resulted in serious problems for Boston. The busy waterfront was packed with overcrowded, disease-filled shacks. Due to the tremendous growth of Catholics in such a short time there were few priests to care for the material and spiritual concerns of the people.

Father Healy courageously visited tuberculosis and cholera victims to administer the last sacraments and to hear confessions. What a surprise when Father Healy answered their calls for a priest. They had never seen a black priest before! But no questions were asked. This priest brought with him Jesus in the Blessed Sacrament. The immigrants, too, were outcasts and eagerly welcomed this dedicated priest.

But not everyone welcomed these new Americans. The growth in numbers of those who believed everyone to be equal except Negroes, Catholics and foreigners compelled Bishop Fitzpatrick to defend the rights of these groups.

A fierce anti-Catholic campaign raged through New England at this time. Churches and schools were looted and burned; the Church and her members were ruthlessly attacked by the press.

"We are Americans, too," Father Healy would say. "We have a right to educate our children and to practice our faith. We can't become discouraged now. There's too much work to be done."

In the early days of 1866, it was evident that Bishop Fitzpatrick would not live much longer. His frail and almost paralyzed body could do no more. His chosen successor, Father Williams, was approved by Pope Pius IX shortly after Bishop Fitzpatrick's death and consecrated as the new bishop.

With the change of bishops, Father Healy was replaced by his brother, Father Sherwood Healy, as chancellor. At the age of thirty-five, this shy black priest, who once worried if his people would accept him, was named the pastor of Boston's second largest parish.

Father Healy's love for children would later earn him the title "the children's bishop." Many afternoons he sat with the children, asking them questions from their catechism, always rewarding right answers with candy or a story. Father Healy, who had been an avid sportsman as a boy, would amuse the children with stories of his boyhood antics.

To a group of admiring altar boys, Father James once recounted: "I was born and grew up in Georgia and never saw a pair of ice skates until my first winter at Holy

On June 10, 1854, Notre Dame was alive with majestic splendor. Its organ thundered throughout the cathedral as the ordination rite commenced. The Archbishop of Paris placed his hands on James' head: "You are a priest forever."

Cross! I considered myself quite a sportsman, until I fell on the ice and couldn't get up without my classmates' pulling me up!"

In November of 1874, the bishop of Portland died suddenly. Three months later, at the age of forty-four, Father Healy was appointed the new bishop whose vast diocese included New Hampshire and Maine.

There were many different sheep in Bishop Healy's new fold. Those for whom he felt the greatest concern were the Abnaki Indians. These people were forced to live on small, unproductive stretches of land. On his first pastoral visit, these devout Catholics welcomed their new bishop with songs and colorful dances.

With them Bishop Healy stressed the universality of the Church. He said that no man should be rejected because of the color of his skin, a subject very close to him.

Traveling north by canoe, the bishop reached the settlements of the French Catholics who fled from Canada to practice their faith. Stepping from the canoe, the bishop was deeply moved to see crowds from miles around gathered to welcome him. Lines of carefully dressed altar boys, who were more used to leather breeches than fine robes, joined in a hearty "Bon jour!"

Bishop Healy thanked his flock in flawless French for the joyous welcome, causing endless delight. His people marveled at his simplicity, barely noticing the color of his skin.

In his pastoral visit, Bishop Healy discovered a shocking witness to religious bigotry—the burned ruins of a parish church.

"We must rebuild at once," the bishop decided firmly.

"But," replied the dismayed pastor, "won't they just come back again? Maybe a few miles away or outside of town?"

"No!" he replied. "We will rebuild here to show that we have the right to practice our faith. Our people must not be deprived of the sacraments. We must show that we are free Americans, too!" With that, the rebuilding of the church was begun.

The year 1900 was a memorable year. In Rome, the Pope opened the Holy Year door in the Eternal City. It was the year of jubilee, inviting all Christians to Rome, to the Chair of St. Peter.

For Bishop Healy, 1900 was also to be a jubilee year. For twenty-five years he had served as the bishop of Portland. On the memorable day, June 5, a procession of hundreds of priests, brothers and sisters filed into the Portland Cathedral. Bishops throughout the East, including Archbishop Williams of Boston, came to honor the aged bishop.

All the seats in the Cathedral were filled, and on the streets outside, the congregation stood to join in the great joy of their bishop.

Bishop Healy himself slowly mounted the pulpit to deliver the homily. With simplicity he thanked God for His goodness and mercies. He then recounted a short history of the Church's struggles in New England, a history he had lived.

What a panorama of events James Healy's life presented. That slight figure who stood so small at the altar lived a volume of history. Born a slave, he had witnessed racial bigotry; as a priest he felt the full impact of religious prejudice; as a bishop, he felt the cross of his responsibility. He had served numerous immigrants; he consoled many families who had lost sons in the Civil War. Most treasured to him, he had seen the Church he served so faithfully grow to vast proportions. Schools, colleges, missions, and charitable institutions, born of so many prayers and sacrifices, now dotted New England.

16

God's regiment

It was January 2, 1863, the height of the bloody Civil War. At Galveston the pre-dawn Texas air hung heavy with gunpowder. Bullets whizzed over the heads of two wounded confederate soldiers lying on the frozen ground. One of them who had been shot in the face propped himself up on his elbows and glanced down the line. Suddenly he spotted something.

"Tom!" he exclaimed to his companion. "What in the name of Jeff Davis are those women doin' down there? They're sure to get killed."

Tom turned a little. Placidly he remarked, "No need to fret, Will. They're sisters lookin' for us wounded. They're not afraid of anythin'."

After the battle, Will hobbled down to the Ursuline convent-turned-army hospital, a short distance away. He himself describes his impressions: "(I saw) the boys in blue and the boys in gray. They treated them all alike, didn't make any difference to them—they were suffering brothers. They had picked up Negroes that had got shot and had them laid out there too. The doctors had more than they could do, and mightly little help except the sisters. One of them held the basin under my face while the doctor was dressing my wound, and she wasn't excited a bit.... I wrote my mother that what we heard about Catholics was far from the truth, and she, like myself, was ever grateful for the good sisters' care of me."

When President Lincoln of the Union and President Davis of the Confederacy called for volunteers for the front lines, they did not recruit only those destined for military uniform. Hundreds of women dedicated to God and the need of their wounded brothers answered the call to arms in the uniforms of their religious habits. Dominicans, Franciscans and members of several other orders spent months, even years, lightening both physical and spiritual loads for all those ravaged by war, regardless of race, army or creed. Some even gave their own lives on the battlefields or in the fever wards, thus completing with their own offering the sacrifice of those they served.

As both nurses and mothers to all, the sisters lavished comfort and aid on those who, unflinching in the face of a cannon, could not face death on a bed.

One little drummer boy in Kentucky's Louisville General Hospital was going fast. A Sister of Charity of the order of Mother Seton bent over the child as he whispered, "I want my mother."

"Sure you do, lamb. Small wonder, too."

"Sister, put your head...on my pillow..., please? I'll believe...you're my mother."

As only children know how, he tucked his thin hand under her black cap and began to pat his "mother's" neck. Gradually the strokes became more irregular until he closed his eyes, only to open them for his Blessed Mother in heaven.

For many suffering soldiers, the nuns were their first contact with Catholicism. And for these many, often an abrupt change in attitude followed—consoling fruits for the sisters' labor.

"Sister," a young officer groaned to one of the "holy ladies," as the nuns were called.

The Sister of Mercy turned.

"Sister, I have to ask you something."

"Yes, John, but be careful. Doctor says that if you want to get well, you shouldn't talk too much."

"Oh, Sister," John murmured, smiling, "you know I already have one foot in the grave."

"Well," she reminded him, "for that matter we all do. It's the common fate of man, you know." Then she added gently, "But what is this question you wanted to ask me?"

The young man hesitated a moment, as a look of uncertainty crossed his face. Then he blurted out, "Sister, how much are you paid?"

The unusual question startled the good nun at first. Then she answered, "But, John, the sisters don't receive any pay."

"No pay?" he gasped. "Not even a cent?"

"No," she replied, "not even a cent. You see, we work for love of God, instead of money."

John glanced from the peaceful eyes of his nurse to the sea of pain around him: men writhing in agony, beads of perspiration on their hot foreheads, while gentle hands of nuns bathed their wounds. Then he began:

"Down where I come from, Sister, they all think Catholics are bad people. We never met many and I guess…" He paused. Then suddenly he bolted up in bed and began to command the sister beside him as he had once ordered soldiers on the battlefield.

"Sister, kindly tell the Catholic chaplain to report to Lieutenant's headquarters immediately."

She returned "on the double," with the priest following.

"Father," Lieutenant John announced, "I called you to enlist me in that army where these nuns serve us suffering prisoners of war for God's own love."

Minutes after the Sister of Mercy witnessed John's initiation into the Church, she witnessed his union with His Supreme Commander in Holy Communion and then his entrance into eternal glory. Weeks later (a victim of fever and love) she, too, answered the same summons as had Lieutenant John.

Yes, the work was hard and the consolations few. Beds had to be changed, clothes washed and mended, food prepared, wounds dressed. Doctors needed help in surgery, and occasional cranky patients pleaded for understanding and care. More often than not, the sister-nurses could squeeze in only a few hours' rest between shifts.

One Sister of Charity recalled:

"Our constant companions were blood and ether, and scalpels replaced the more familiar kitchen knives. On one sticky afternoon these proved to be too much for me. I felt faint and had to rush out into the clean air and sunshine. But something brought me back. I thought of the wound in my Lord's side and I found the strength I needed to return to the wounds in my soldiers' tortured limbs."

Faith's steady flame,
continually fed with
prayer and the Eucharist,
consumed them
and ignited others.

In the humdrum routine of daily living and working, these recruits in God's regiment sanctified their efforts, successes and failures, by offering them through, with, in, and to Jesus, so that everything became not just work, but an apostolate, a mission. In the battered bodies of their soldiers they saw the image of their crucified Savior. Tending *their* ills, they tended His, and restoring *them* to health, they helped Him to conquer death once more. Faith's steady flame, continually fed with prayer and the Eucharist, consumed them and ignited others.

One evening, as the autumn sun cast lengthening shadows on the Stanton Hospital in Washington, D.C., a group of Mercy Sisters spied a tall, lanky silhouette against the crimson sky. With simplicity and courtesy, Abraham Lincoln, himself a man of deep faith, greeted the sisters:

"Would you welcome an old man to your home tonight, Sister?"

"No," Mother Rose smiled. "But we do welcome you, Mr. President. Would you care to visit the sick?"

As Lincoln wandered among the rows of clean hospital cots, the Mason-Dixon line gradually disappeared, and he exchanged words with Union and Confederate victims alike:

"Are the sisters good to you, son?"

"No, sir. They're better than that...."

"No more cold peas at front lines for a while, right, Captian?"

"For forever, I hope, Mr. Lincoln.... And I thought *Ma* was a good cook...."

Later, after many visits to the hospital, Lincoln paid this glowing tribute to the sister-nurses of the Civil War:

"Of all the forms of charity and benevolence seen in the crowded wards of the hospitals, those of some Catholic Sisters were among the most efficient. I never knew whence they came.... More lovely than anything I had ever seen in art, so long devoted to illustrations of love, mercy and charity, are the pictures that remain of these modest Sisters going on their errands of mercy among the suffering and the dying, gentle and womanly, yet with the courage of soldiers.... As they went from cot to cot, distributing the medicines prescribed, administering the cooling, refreshing, strengthening (drafts) as directed, they were veritable Angels of Mercy. Their words were suited to every sufferer. One they incited or encouraged, another they calmed and soothed. With every soldier they conversed about his home, his wife, his children, all the loved ones he was soon to see again if he were obedient and patient. How many times have I seen them exorcise pain by their presence or their words! How often has the hot forehead of the soldier grown cool as one of these Sisters bathed it! How often has he been refreshed, encouraged and assisted along the road to convalescence when he would otherwise have fallen by the way, by some home memories with which these unpaid nurses filled the heart."

In the mid-nineteenth century no Red Cross volunteers or Army Nurses Corps were around to relieve the burden of the battlefield or the unsanitary conditions of the army hospitals. But their predecessors, the "Angels of Mercy," *did* render service and *did* give to many, new hope for the future. In peace and obscurity they never sought the acclaim of this world, although many testified to their generous commitment.

When an army officer asked a helper in the Kentucky Sisters of Charity hospital about the nuns' political sympathies, the wise woman declared, "Suh, de Sistahs ain't fo' de Souf nuh fo' de Noif; dey's fo' God."

17

the thirst

The year was 1869; the country, Ireland. A burly dock hand called: "Hey, errand boy! Come over here! What's your name? How old are you?"

"Matthew Talbot and I'm thirteen, sir. Do you have a message for me to take somewhere?"

"Well...no. How long now have you been working here?"

"Two weeks, sir. But it's a little boring; there aren't too many messages to deliver."

The man laughed to himself and rubbed his chin as he said: "Some of us have decided to initiate you and make you one of us. Here's a bottle. This is what *we men* do around here when we're bored."

"But where did you get that?" Matt asked.

"This is a wine place, isn't it? A case broke and this is what's left over."

Matt started to turn and go. He didn't want anything to do with this drinking business. The Talbots never drank at home. What would his mother and father say?

The man chided him and said, "What's the matter? ...Ea, Matty? Maybe you're still too young to drink!! We could put some milk in a cup for you instead."

Matt stopped and turned. His face was scarlet as he blurted out,

"I'm not afraid to drink. It's just that I don't care for it right now."

The man just laughed. The boy debated within himself and then said,

"I'll take one drink, okay? Just to be social and prove to you I'm not afraid."

Less than a year later Matthew Talbot was not only drinking to be sociable; he was drunk most of the time. Rumors started to spread throughout the city, and gossip usually travels at a gallop.

"Did you see that young Talbot yesterday? Why, he's a disgrace, such a little drunkard. I just happened to look out the window; there he was, reeling and staggering right past my house."

"Imagine, what a heartbreak for his good parents! I've known that family for years. They never miss Mass, and they say the rosary every night together. It's a real shame."

"His father took him out of school. Mr. Talbot earns so little money at his job, and he has twelve mouths to feed. Matt was supposed to help, but I don't think he'll be giving much money to the family now."

"I heard that, too, but I also heard Matthew is the messenger boy of the wine merchants' warehouse."

"Poor Mr. Talbot...he probably blames himself."

"Well, you know that all the men at that place drink heavily. It's their bad example that induced the boy to drink."

The tongues kept on wagging until the gossip reached the ears of Matt's parents. Mrs. Talbot whispered to her husband, "It's almost impossible for me to believe that Matt is resorting to the 'awful drink.'"

Then one evening their son stumbled in the house drunk. Early the next morning, Mr. Talbot changed his son's place of work and took Matt with him to the Ports and Docks Board. Matt became their new messenger boy.

Without realizing it, his father put him into greater temptations. Now the boy found whiskey instead of wine. It was all over the piers. His father scolded him, beat him, begged him to stop, but nothing seemed to help. Matt's parents were heartbroken.

The boy changed his place of work. In this way he would save his father the agony of seeing him in a state of perpetual drunkenness. Matt became a bricklayer. As his parents watched their son's steady downward slide, they suffered and walked their way of the cross, station by station. They prayed.... Oh, how they prayed! Surely God would help him. Meanwhile, the years passed by.

Every weekend after work Matt followed the same schedule. The quitting whistle pierced the air on Saturday evening. It signaled the time for work wages. As the money was passed out, several friends usually gathered together.

"Come on, Matt. Quit counting your money and let's get going. I'm so dry, there's fire in my mouth and only a shot of whiskey can quench it."

"You're right!" Matt replied. "It's just too bad our money only lasts until the beginning of each week. And your money, Pete, runs out quicker than mine."

"That's okay," Pete said, "if mine outlasted yours I would buy you a drink. That's our pact, right?"

Another friend joined in. "Sure, that's right. Whoever has leftover money is obliged to buy drinks 'on the house.' That's what friends are for. Let's get going. This money's so hot I think I'll buy the first round of drinks."

At this they all quickly walked to their favorite bar. No price was too great to pay for a drink. One time Matt sold his boots. Another time he and his buddy tricked a drinking companion. The buddy kept the poor man busy while Matt stole his violin. They pawned it and bought drinks "on the house" for everyone. When the poor man realized the drinks were being served at the cost of his livelihood, he became hopelessly dejected. That didn't matter to Matt. The violin had bought a few drinks. What mattered beyond that?

Yet, there were times when he wanted to stop drinking...to take the pledge and become a good Catholic... but he didn't have the courage.

One week came though, that Matt didn't work, and by Monday he had drunk up the leftover money from the previous week. He craved whiskey with all his being. His whole body seemed to be on fire. Only one thought kept Matt going: Saturday was approaching and his drinking buddies would know what it was like to "go dry," so they would buy him a drink. Sure,...they would help him.

Matt trembled with eagerness as he waited on the familiar corner across from the work yard. The whistle blew. A few men hurried out, laughing and joking. When one noticed Matt, he poked at the others. They fell silent and tried to ignore him, scurrying past without a word. A few more came out of the yard and crossed the street. Matt called to them. They were his best friends!

"Hey, Jim,...Pete! It's me, Matt."

"Oh, Matt.... How have you been? We missed you this week.... Well, we've got to be going. Come to see us when you're working again."

His heart filled with anger...then remorse. It seemed that everything his drinking habit had smothered inside him for years was now coming to the surface. Slowly he made a decision.

"Not one invited me to come and have a drink," Matt said to himself. "It wasn't like this before."

Something icy swelled in his stomach and crept into his throat. He was humiliated. Things were different now. He was broke. It didn't matter to them one bit how badly he needed a drink.

"I always bought drinks for the others when I had money. See, they just took advantage of me! Friendship to them is only as important as the amount of money in your pocket—no money, no friends. Each of them is wrapped up in his own vice. To share a drink with someone who has no money, no matter how bad off he is, only deprives the lender of another shot of whiskey. Who wants to share a drink with a bum?"

His heart filled with anger...then remorse. It seemed that everything his drinking habit had smothered inside him for years was now coming to the surface. Slowly he made a decision. He would take the pledge to stop drinking, and with God's grace, he would keep it. God would be his friend, the only Friend he could be sure of,...the Friend who would never betray him.

Matt was now twenty-eight years old. He had spent more than half his young life drunk. He went home and told his parents, to their great astonishment and joy, about his firm resolution. Then he went to a nearby chapel and made a good confession and took the pledge for three months. It seemed impossible to Matt to abstain from drink for that long; "but with God nothing is impossible."

After his good confession he started to attend daily· Mass and Communion. He became a Franciscan Tertiary and lived a most austere penitential life. Giving up drink was by no means easy. There were many temptations and constant battles to fight and to win. But Matt prayed, and gradually through self-denial and prayer he became stronger and stronger.

By the end of the first three months, the man who had once let alcohol rule his life was now ready to take the total abstinence pledge. Until Matt Talbot's death, some fifty years later, he never took another drink. The man whose tremendous "thirst" had once led him far from God, learned through self-denial and prayer that the only "thirst" that leads to happiness is the thirst for the God who has made us for Himself.

18

nobody's
children...
but
Father
John's

John Drumgoole's heart was beating fast. In the darkness he bowed his head in reverence. And then as he fixed his eyes on the tabernacle before him, he began to pray with a rush of eagerness: "Help me to spend my life doing good, O Lord. Help me to be holy. Help me..." he paused and fixed his eyes on the altar, "to be a worthy priest!"

As he stepped out into the sunlight once more, he blinked several times and looked around. The neighborhood hadn't changed very much. Familiar faces greeted him and hands waved. Busy carriages hurried by and small children dodged skillfully out of their path.

The children.... They were not yesterday's children, many of whom had grown up since John Drumgoole had gone away to the seminary. And yet, in a way, they *were* the same children; abandoned, orphaned, lonely—with cares and concerns too mature for their little hearts to bear.

He crossed the street and knocked at the door of a simple house. Mrs. Kerrigan answered the door after several moments and beheld a thoughtful priest with his head still turned, eyes glued on those children in the street.

"Why, John Drumgoole!" she exclaimed in her heavy Irish brogue, "*Father* John Drumgoole, how proud we are of you! And black never looked better on you than it does this minute!"

Father Drumgoole smiled his happiness, but he seemed to be looking beyond her. "Where is she?" he whispered.

Mrs. Kerrigan beamed and motioned for him to come in. "Bridget!" she called. "The blessings of God are upon the house this day!"

There was a stir in the back room, and from a door at the end of the hall, John saw a tiny figure of a woman appear. The two peered through the darkness in a solemn moment of silence.

"John?" Her voice began to tremble with emotion. "John, is that you, my son?"

Father Drumgoole hurried down the hall to his mother. "Your eyes are as bright as ever, Mother!" the new priest observed. "But she moves so slowly," he thought, "and the years have taken their toll on her strength...."

"And you look fine and healthy, my son," she said. Her mother's pride doted over him. He had been gone for so long.

Her hair was white now, and her skin was wrinkled, but her heart had not changed. She stroked his sleeve and then her experienced hand stopped in incredulity. "But where did you learn to sew like this? The seminary...?"

John Christopher Drumgoole threw back his head and laughed heartily. "No, Mother. The sisters near the seminary did me that courtesy. They are such a good community." He paused, "Mother?"

"Yes, my son, what is it?"

Father Drumgoole strode to the window overlooking the street, and again his eyes met the scene of children running and playing in their vagabond world. "Loretto!" he exclaimed.

Mrs. Drumgoole looked up at him questioningly.

"When I was at the seminary, Mother, and I first met those sisters, I told them all about my desires for the future. See those children out there?" he pointed.

His mother was silent. With her eyes on the floor, she said softly, "Yes, John. Many of them—*most* of them, are homeless—orphaned or abandoned. I, too, have watched at length from that window, but I have had to turn away because I could no longer bear to think of those innocent little creatures—so alone...."

Father Drumgoole smiled, "I will make myself their father! I'll gather them all from wherever I find them and I'll give them a home and call it Mount Loretto after those sisters of Loretto...." His face was flushed with excitement as the fruits of long hours of prayer and thought poured enthusiastically from his lips.

On Sunday, May 30, 1869, Father John Christopher Drumgoole said his first Mass. From the front pew, Bridget Drumgoole watched her son through mother's eyes that could not help but fill with tears.

The new priest was fifty-two years old; his hair was just beginning to gray. At the time in life when most laborers in the vineyard are well underway in their efforts, Father John was just beginning his. He had not avoided his calling. Delay was due to the patient, plodding efforts of this Irish immigrant to get an education while supporting himself and his mother by working as a cobbler, sexton and bookseller. It had been a long, hard struggle, Bridget reminisced, but now John stood at the altar where he had always yearned to be.

Father Drumgoole had not long begun his work with his beloved children in a house on Warren Street when God asked of him one of the greatest sacrifices of his life.

It was a stifling August day in 1874. Father John sat beside his mother's bed. Her breathing was shallow. In a small, trembling voice, she said, "John? All your boys... I'm going to let our Blessed Mother know what good care you take of your boys...."

"And what good care you took of me, Mother," Father John reminded her tenderly. Bridget Drumgoole closed her eyes and silently passed into the world of eternity.

Father Drumgoole resolved to be a father to every homeless child. And with the permission and blessing of the bishop of New York City, his home for the little ones at 55 Warren Street grew. He took in any children that came, and he went out himself in search of those who were too shy to come on their own: all lonely children, abandoned children, orphans.

Soon, too soon, the home became too small. Rather than refuse to receive any more boys, Father John chose to improve the building. But not even in the late 1800's did money grow on trees. What could he do?

Father Drumgoole turned to St. Joseph, who knew well what providing meant. Joseph had had a foster Child to care for, too! On a rickety chair in Father's room, a statue of the saint was placed, and in his simplicity, Father John would have heart-to-heart talks with his patron. He told him of his successes and failures—and his concerns. In those days when the economy was tight, Father John felt the burden of his nearly two hundred boys. Space was a luxury, too. Many a night passed when little boys had to sleep on the floor because there just weren't enough beds to go around. But Father John Drumgoole never lost his trust in God. He tried to seek God's kingdom first, and with a patron like St. Joseph he was *sure* the rest would follow.

His hopes were not deluded. Funds were donated to repair and improve the shabby Home on Warren Street—enough for a chapel that could hold two hundred and fifty boys, an airy classroom, a gym, a lecture hall, and individual sleeping cubicles. Father John furnished each cubicle with a little locker and a wash basin. He firmly believed in giving his boys a sense of confidence and responsibility.

"Where do all the boys come from?" an open-mouthed reporter once asked him.

The priest ran his hand through his gray hair, and smiled, puzzled. "No one knows. I guess they just fall from the clouds." He had never cared where the boys came from. Their future was his main concern.

One day a little boy approached one of the regular boarders at the home. "Kin I git in?" he queried shyly. "My friend Tim says it's full.... I don't have anywhere ilse to go."

The other boy promptly put his arm around the hesitant orphan and said reassuringly, "C'mon! Father John'll hang you up somewhere."

Father John accepted all children—white or black. "There are no color barriers in this home," he said. They were all God's children whose bodies needed to be fed and whose souls desperately starved for something more —*love.* There was no love for them on the streets of New York City, dodging carriages, picking through garbage cans and taking turns sleeping on outdoor heat registers when the nights were cold and their little bodies, numb.

Father Drumgoole took in as many as he could during the winter cold, even though there was literally no space left. While the night wind slashed and snapped at the trees, little children peacefully slept inside—on benches in the dining room, on the rugs in the parlor. They knew they had found a friend.

The expenses of one winter again found Father John in debt. He continued his anxious conversations before the statue of St. Joseph propped up on the chair. And his faith was not wasted. A loan was given to him with no interest asked—and another check of sizable amount was sent to him by the Irish immigrant society.

Father John's talks with St. Joseph brought about another new growth—a house on Lafayette Street—eight stories high. It was one of the tallest buildings in New York at the time. Before the year of 1881 was over, that marvelous home, too, was filled to capacity. There was one special thing about Father John: he just couldn't say "no."

John Christopher Drumgoole lay feverishly ill. The anxious faces that surrounded him were those of the sisters he had brought to help him in the home, and the doctor. It was 1888—during the great blizzard in New York.

"He is only a shell," the doctor had declared. "He is completely worked out."

"*Now* you trust *me* to take care of you," he had told his children just a few days earlier, "but when I'm gone and there is no one to turn to, go to St. Joseph. He never failed me, not once in my life. I know he will never fail you either."

What was going on in the mind of this old priest who had been a father to so many? No doubt he was thinking of the only love of his life…his children. In the years that had spanned the second home on Lafayette Street, he had begun the third home—this one on Staten Island—a sprawling farm-home which he had finally named Mount

Loretto. Here children became healthy; pale, drawn little faces, tanned and frail arms and legs grew strong. And as he had always done before, Father Drumgoole helped all these children grow closer to God, who, they were told, was truly their very own Father in heaven.

He had cared for over 160,000 children, and fed and clothed thousands of other poor people. But he had sought no earthly honors. These were merely sand in comparison to the treasures he had earned for the life to come.

"Father John," the doctor was saying, "I'm afraid that death is near...." His voice trailed off. "There is nothing more I can do."

The seventy-one-year-old priest blinked and raised his eyes to heaven. "Then, God's will be done." He raised a feeble arm to the window. "I hoped I would live longer. There is so much to be done for my boys.... But God's will be done."

That afternoon Archbishop Corrigan came to see Father John. He found a still, white form, motionless on the bed. "I see you have St. Joseph very near to you," he said kindly.

Father John looked up at the pictures of St. Joseph on the bed. "Oh, I couldn't live without him—or die without him."

As the prayers for the dying were being said, Father John's hand suddenly relaxed on the rosary beads he had been clasping. He went home to his God, whom he had served so tirelessly on earth. He had once said that the more destitute and miserable the children were when he met them, the more they resembled Christ. And now he would receive from Christ the welcome to an eternal reward.

19

hell transformed

Hawaii! The land of palm trees and coconuts, of flowers and vibrant color, was a tropical paradise long before it became the fiftieth state. If one were going to Honolulu, Hawaii meant beauty, relaxation and a friendly atmosphere. However, if one were going to Molokai, it meant *despair!*

The island of Molokai, in the center of the Hawaiian chain, was a desolate region. On its rugged surface, nearly 2,000 men, women and children lived in total isolation. Forced to leave their homes and families, they had come to the village of Kalaupapa to waste away and die. Society considered them outcasts, for they had contracted what was then considered the most terrible disease known to man—leprosy!

The plight of those forgotten people moved the heart of Bishop Maigret. On May 4, 1873, the bishop spoke with several missionary priests at Wailúku, on the island of Maui.

"Reverend Fathers, I had decided to grant the requests of the lepers of Molokai to have their own resident priest. But...I cannot lay this burden on any of you; it would be like sentencing a man to death."

At this point, a rugged young missionary jumped to his feet.

"I...I want to go, Your Excellency!"

"Damien, do you realize what kind of assignment you're volunteering for?"

"Yes, Bishop, I do. I still want to go; I am ready to embrace their lot and prison of death."

"Thank you, my son! You've lifted a great weight from my heart. When can you be ready?"

"I'm ready now, Your Excellency."

"Good! You can leave on the next boat in six days; and I'll accompany you myself and introduce you to your new children."

The boat had docked, and Father Damien sank his feet into Molokai's sandy shore.

"I am here for life," he said to himself. "I am on Molokai forever. I will die here—on this island."

Because of the Board of Health regulations, anyone who went to Molokai had to remain there for the rest of his life.

However, to the thirty-three-year-old priest with only nine years of missionary experience behind him, the future gleamed with brightness. Full of energy, strength and enthusiasm, Father Damien was willing to sacrifice himself completely, for he was driven by a force greater than man: the force of divine love.

Upon his arrival in the village, the young priest's eyes met with a most pitiful spectacle. The people who greeted him resembled, not human beings, but corpses, devoured by worms. Bloated and covered with sores, they exhaled a stench so great that it seemed to have come from an opened grave.

A large wooden door creaked open. As Father Damien stepped into the one-room leprosarium, his reaction was one of utter shock.

"This is the hospital?" he exclaimed.

There were no doctors, no beds. Lying on the floor, stretched out on mats, were hundreds of lepers, suffering from cold and hunger. Water was scarce, flies swarmed everywhere, and the sick simply wallowed in filth.

As the young missionary's eyes circled the room, he said to himself: "These unfortunate ones are now my spiritual children...and I, in turn, am to be their father."

Immediately, Father Damien began to care for the material and especially the spiritual needs of the lepers. It was with much difficulty that he carried out his duties, however, for every fiber of his being rebelled against the conditions in which he found himself.

In performing his priestly ministry—baptizing, hearing confessions, distributing Holy Communion and anointing the sick—Father Damien was compelled to hold his nose, or even to run outside periodically to catch a breath of fresh air. The stench of leprous sweat nauseated him, and the fluid that leaked from the open sores caused his legs to itch so badly that he had to wear high boots in order to prevent it. His clothes, too, carried the odor of leprosy, so he tried to counteract it by constantly smoking a pipe.

"Lord, give me strength, courage, charity..." Damien prayed. "Let me help my people more, love them more, and forget myself."

Even though his senses rebelled at the encounter with each deformed person, Father Damien persisted in his work among the lepers. He strove to always be cheerful, although his eyes burned at the sight of them, his ears split with their shrieks of anguish, and his touch froze from contact with their rotting skin.

Every step brought the revelation of new miseries, but the zealous missionary accepted this as an opportunity to love these people more, to do penance and to show his love for God.

His prayers were constant, for the strength he needed was a grace that God alone can give.

And these prayers were answered. God opened his eyes, his hands, and his heart to see all the needs of his brothers. He abandoned himself ever more completely in order to be of greater service to others.

Father Damien saw that, besides the wounds of the body, these lepers experienced a more tremendous suffering—that of the soul. There was moral ruin everywhere. Not only were the people discouraged by the disgust they aroused, but the torments of the disease drove away all hope, and they found nothing to live for.

The missionary knew what was lacking in the lives of some of these lepers: it was faith, hope and love. Despised by all, many thought that even God hated them, and as a result they broke every divine law, collapsing into impurity, idolatry and utter brutality.

By his example and witness in following Christ, Father Damien uplifted the morality of the entire island. The lepers called him "Makna," which means "Father," for he was always giving to his children. He built houses for them, taught them to raise crops, gave them food, clothing and medicine, dressed their wounds, arranged recreational activities, and even organized them into an orchestra.

By creating such activities, the pastor helped to rid his people of idleness, and enabled them to discover the spirit of Christian joy.

Father Damien's greatest happiness, however, was found in teaching the little ones their catechism, for he wanted more than anything else to lead them along the way to heaven. The children learned well and tried their best to put into practice everything their pastor taught them. They even attended daily Mass and Benediction.

One day, upon returning home from an errand, Father Damien found one of the leper girls sitting outside the door of his cabin.

"Are you waiting for me, Tatila?" he asked.

"Yes, Father," she answered. "Please bring me Holy Communion. Please bring it to me right now."

Without any further question, the priest brought to the child the Blessed Sacrament, which she devoutly received. No sooner had she finished thanking Jesus who had come into her heart, than she went to meet Him in heaven.

The following day, Father Damien made her small coffin and dug her grave, as he had done for all the lepers who died.

As months turned into years, the Apostle of Molokai progressed in his love for and devotion to the lepers. Even when dressing the most loathsome sores, Father Damien looked as though he were arranging a bouquet of flowers, completely forgetful of himself and of the repugnance he felt.

One poor leper in the last stages of the disease, looked up to see the good priest changing the soiled bandages around his waist.

"Oh, Father," he exclaimed. "Please take greater precautions. My wounds are leaking much—the fluid will get on your hands."

"That's all right, Joseph," the priest replied. "I don't mind it. It's more important that you have clean bandages."

"But you can get leprosy. You know that the last stages of the disease are the most contagious."

"Don't be so disturbed, my son. Even if the disease seizes my body, God will give me a better one on resurrection day. Isn't the all-important thing the saving of one's soul? By doing this now, I am working to save my soul, and yours, too. It is our sanctification that God wills, and that is what we must all strive to attain on this earth."

One day in 1884, forty-four-year-old Father Damien sat alone in his cabin. He plunged his feet into a basin of boiling water.... He felt no pain! This experiment was to remove all uncertainty. As he withdrew his feet, he saw them covered with large blisters, as ribbons of skin began to shrivel away.

Now he knew beyond doubt that he too was a leper!

The disease made rapid progress. Large blisters appeared on his once handsome face, and his neck became red and bloated. The powerful hands that had worked so tirelessly for others were now covered with swellings and sores.

"Why don't you go home and breathe your native air for a while?" the doctor strongly recommended.

"But what would become of my wretched children here?" the leper priest replied.

"But you must think of yourself, too."

"No, I will not. I—I must not! These people need a pastor. They need someone to care for their souls. Since there is so much opportunity for doing good here, I will remain at my post until—until I die, if it is the will of God."

Back in Belgium Father Damien's family tried to conceal the news from his mother. She was eighty-three years old now and her health was failing. A gossipy neighbor broke the harsh news to Madame de Veuster.

"Look at your son," the woman's shrill voice screeched as she shook a newspaper in front of Mrs. de Veuster.

Madame de Veuster wept a long time and then said, "Well, I shall soon go to heaven with my Joseph. Flesh of my flesh, my handsome, courageous boy! So affectionate, so dear to me. My son!"

Father Damien's mother choked back her tears and said to one of her children, "How much he must be suffering, alone on a deserted island, dying by such slow torture; oh, if only I could embrace him, kiss my boy and comfort him!"

On April 6, 1886, Mama de Veuster died peacefully after one last, loving gaze upon *her* Joseph's picture.

For three more years, Father Damien worked vigorously for the bodies and the souls of his beloved lepers.

Far from quenching his zeal, the leprosy seemed to make it blaze ever more vibrantly. Trials were many, and the fatigue and suffering became more intense with each new day, yet he bore all for the love of Christ who had died on the cross for him, and for all people.

On April 13, 1889, a few days before Easter, Father Damien gave his soul back to God. His work was finished. He had transformed the hell of Molokai into a haven of God's love. Father Damien did not only die a victim of leprosy. He died a victim of sacrifice because of his love for Christ, and for the souls of God's least ones, the lepers of Molokai.

20

longer
than
the longest
life

Zelie Martin sat upright in the chair of the doctor's office on that never-to-be-forgotten day in 1876. She waited patiently for his verdict. Without raising his eyes, the doctor cleared his throat and began writing out a prescription. He said, "Madame, what you have is a tumor."

"Be frank with me, Doctor. What is the use of the prescription?"

"Really no use at all, Mrs. Martin," admitted the doctor.

"Will...will an operation help me?"

"I'm afraid not, Madame. It is too late. You've come to see a doctor many years too late."

Dazed, Zelie stood up, mumbled words of thanks to the doctor and slowly made her way home. Home was a comfortable house in Alençon, France, where her husband was a jeweler and she herself had a small lace-making business. Zelie prepared a good dinner for her husband and five daughters that night. The visit to the doctor had been made alone and she alone knew the dreadful truth about her illness.

Exteriorly she was the same Zelie. But her heart was torn with anguish. "What will poor Louis do without me?" she thought. "What will happen to Marie, Pauline, my problem child Leonie, Celine and baby Thérèse? How will they manage when I'm not here? It seems impossible that I can die of this. I must remain for a little while longer. I will live!"

Supper time arrived and everything was ready. Papa Martin led his family in prayer and everyone sat down to Mama's delicious meal. Three-year-old Thérèse sat perched on her high chair happily fingering her fork and spoon. Mama swallowed hard as she looked at her baby and rose to get more milk.

After supper was over and the dishes were washed, the family gathered in the living room as usual. It was then that Mama told them the bad news. The scene was heartrending. Poor Louis just sat in his armchair, his unlit pipe laying in his lap where it had fallen. He looked from Zelie to the circle of children and back to his wife. The three oldest girls, Marie, Pauline and Leonie, sobbed inconsolably. Leonie, Zelie's problem child who had been expelled from school three times, ran to fling her arms around her mother's neck. She knew her mother would understand her unspoken words. Little Celine and Thérèse looked very puzzled and wondered what this was all about. They had never seen everyone so sad before.

Mama alone was dry-eyed. After a few moments, she donned an apron and cheerfully set about doing some work. Her calmness and serenity eventually managed to quiet the other members of the family a little. Zelie would not let her devoted husband and children see the ache in her own heart.

The busy round of household tasks and the prosperous lace-making business which she conducted in her home continued as usual. Zelie's greatest preoccupation, however, was her children's welfare and the burden that would fall on her beloved husband's shoulders. He would have to be both mother and father to the girls when she was gone. In a letter to her sister-in-law, Zelie wrote:

"I am very far from being under any illusions. And I can scarcely sleep at night when I think of the future of my children.... All the same, I am doing my best, with God's help, to be resigned, though I was far from expecting such a trial.... I have had my severe trials in life, but this is hard to face.... Louis is inconsolable. He has lost his pleasure in fishing and has put away his rods in the attic; he no longer cares to go to his club. He is as though completely crushed...."

At the age of forty-five, Zelie Martin had brought nine children into the world. But of these, two boys and two girls had died in her arms. Each new death had cut her deeply and had increased her longing to join her little angels in heaven. Yes, heaven. She had always lived for heaven even though she had been completely absorbed in her duties as a wife and mother.

Often her mind flew back seventeen years to a day when she and Louis had discussed their plans for their first baby, soon to arrive, and she had asked, "Louis, do you think I am selfish to want my child to become a saint? I don't mean a canonized saint, of course, just a saint in God's eyes. I want my children to lead holy lives, and I hope all of them will. Is that too much to ask of the good Lord in my prayers?"

Calm and dependable, Louis had answered, "Of course you're not selfish, Zelie dearest. Every parent should want his or her child to become a saint, and everyone should aspire to sainthood—even you and I. Trying to become saints by doing God's will, even in the smallest matters, is what makes the most humdrum life a glorious challenge. I hope we can teach our children these things, Zelie."

Enthusiastically she concluded, "In planning for our children's future, Louis, I'm going to try to keep in mind the joys of heaven which await us. Heaven will be much longer than the longest life on earth and its joys deeper than the deepest joy of this world. You and I, Louis, and all our children must be together in heaven to enjoy the beatific vision forever."

In the years that followed, she had really tried to live for heaven. True, there had been many moments of human weakness, but she and Louis had always found strength in praying together and with their children. They had formed the habit of gathering around the fire-place in the evening to read some spiritual book before going to bed. Celine, the fourth youngest, would write in later years:

"My mother and father possessed deep faith. When we heard them talking together of eternity, and reading aloud certain passages from *Imitation of Christ*, we were led, young as we were, to look upon the things of this world as vanity."

With her health slipping fast, Zelie Martin set about fulfilling her duties with a zest and enthusiasm that amazed everyone. One day someone remarked, "Madame Martin, you certainly must be a valiant woman to undergo such great sufferings with a smile."

"No!" exclaimed Zelie. "I am not virtuous enough to desire great sufferings. I dread them. I am trying to convert myself but I cannot succeed. At times, I really feel discouraged. Yet, it is God who makes the saints, and He can do for us in one moment what we cannot accomplish in days or years."

In a later letter to her sister-in-law, Zelie confided: "God is giving me the grace not to be frightened.... I am very peaceful! I feel almost happy! If God wills to cure me, I shall be glad; for it is only natural that in my heart I want to live. It costs me much to leave my husband and children. But, on the other hand, I feel that if I am not cured, it will be because, perhaps, it is better for me that I go.... God knows best...." Just two months before her death, Zelie dragged herself to Lourdes in the fervent hope of obtaining a miracle.

When the courageous woman returned to Alençon, Louis stood anxiously on the platform, holding the hands of his youngest daughters, Celine and Thérèse. As soon as the youngsters saw their mother, they jumped for joy and ran to throw their arms around her neck. Zelie winced in pain, and Louis caught it. Yet, she smiled as cheerfully as though she had received the desired cure.

To sixteen-year-old Pauline, who had prayed so fervently for the big miracle and who felt so very disappointed, Mrs. Martin said soothingly, "Do not hope too much for joys on earth, dear. Our Lady of Lourdes says to us as she said to Bernadette, 'I do not promise to make you happy in this world, but in the next.' As for me, I know from experience how little one may count upon earthly joys; and if I did not hope for the joys of heaven, I would be a very unhappy woman."

A month later, when the family sat down to a Sunday meal which the dying mother had insisted on preparing herself, her brother Isadore, a pharmicist, cleared his throat and made a statement out of what he felt was his duty. "My poor sister," he said, "you must not be under any illusions. Set your affairs in order for you have no more than a month to live."

Shocked, Louis dropped his fork and gasped. Controlling his emotions he spoke only a few words of reproval to his inconsiderate brother-in-law, who could not have chosen a more inopportune time to inform Zelie of her condition—right there at the table in front of all the children. Marie, Pauline, Leonie, and Celine sat in a stupor and looked from their uncle to their mother to their poor distraught father. Only little Thérèse kept on eating.

Zelie, who had always wanted truthfulness and frankness in regard to her condition, managed a weak, sad smile of gratitude. Later, when Zelie was alone with Isadore, the poor man stammered, "I'm sorry, Zelie. I'm sorry I told you that and in the way I did...."

Smiling gently, Zelie comforted, "Don't worry about it, Isadore. I am very grateful for your frankness; after all, I had asked you to tell me the truth. As I told your dear wife, I have faced the situation squarely and am trying to live as though I am to die. I mustn't waste the short time I have remaining to me. These days are days of salvation which will never return and I want to profit by them. I shall gain doubly, for in resigning myself to the will of God, I shall suffer less, and I shall also do a portion of my purgatory here on earth."

In the last seven weeks of her illness, Zelie was filled with excruciating pain. The slightest movement or noise was sheer torture. Feverish and sometimes delirious, she would cry out, "Oh, you who made me! Have mercy on me! Oh, my God! You see that my strength to suffer is leaving me! Have pity on me! I beseech You, do not forsake me!"

On two Sundays, Zelie pulled herself up from bed and stubbornly made her way to church. To the protests of her husband and children, she answered, "I am not ill enough to miss Mass on Sunday." At every step of the way, pain shot through her. But she did assist at Mass although she could barely sit or kneel.

Afterwards she went to confession. Deeply moved, the Abbe Crete could not hold back words of admiration for this courageous woman: "Madame, I have seen some brave women, but never one like you!"

A few weeks later, Mrs. Martin was anointed. Louis knelt beside the bed, completely overcome with grief. All five daughters knelt silently by, crying. Zelie could no longer speak. She could only fix a long look of supplication upon her young sister-in-law, who understood.

Zelie Martin passed into eternity at 12:30 AM on August 28, 1877, at the age of forty-six. All five of her daughters would offer themselves totally to God in the cloistered religious life and the youngest would one day be known as St. Therese of the Child Jesus, the Little Flower. Of her mother, St. Thérèse said,

"The good God did me the favor of awakening my intelligence when I was still very young.... Perhaps He wished, in His love, to have me know and appreciate the incomparable mother He had given me. As I grew older, my love of God deepened and I frequently offered God my heart, using the words which Mama had taught me...."

21

**God's
candle**

"Daddy," little Francesca asked, "guess what I did today!"

Agostino Cabrini set his dark-haired seven-year-old on his lap.

"What?"

"I made little paper boats and sailed them downstream to China!"

"To China?" Agostino asked.

"Oh yes, Papa. Just like in those mission stories that you read to us. I love stories that tell about missionaries. Daddy, *what is a missionary?*"

"Well, Francesca, a missionary is a person who loves God so much that he or she wants to tell everybody about Him. Some people leave their families and friends and even their country to go to lands far away and spread Jesus' love everywhere. Isn't that great?"

"It sure is! You know, Daddy, maybe I'll be a missionary some day!"

Mr. Cabrini laughed, ruffled his daughter's curly black hair and mumbled: "No doubt about it...no doubt about it!"

Years passed. Francesca became Mother Frances Xavier Cabrini, Foundress of the Missionaries of the Sacred Heart.

The dreams and hopes nurtured since childhood—to take Christ's message to China—filled Mother Cabrini's soul as she went into St. Peter's Basilica in Rome to pray. First she talked to the Master about the needs of the people in another place...far-off America. Of course, she wanted to help them, too—as some people thought she should—but how could she do two things at once? After all, she had always intended to spend her life doing God's work in the Orient. Then, a private audience with the great Pontiff, Leo XIII, changed the whole course of her life! Pope Leo said with conviction: "You must not go to the East, but to the West. Your mission will be in America to help the thousands of Italian immigrants there and to make your native country loved."

Mother Cabrini had gone to Rome unknown and without any influential "human" help; in a few days she would be leaving Rome with valuable letters of recommendation. Now she was ready to begin her work in America. The Foundress and six of her sisters sailed for America on the feast of St. Joseph—March 19, 1889. Sister Frances Xavier Cabrini was then thirty-nine years old.

The *Bourgogne* sailed into New York harbor on March 31. Mother Cabrini glowed with anticipation as she and the sisters were taken by the kindly Scalabrini Fathers to St. Joachim's rectory. After the Italian-style dinner prepared just for them, Mother Cabrini asked: "Will you take us to our own convent now, Fathers?"

The priests glanced nervously at each other, and then the pastor said in halting phrases, "The convent... oh, yes...the convent...to be sure. We tried to find a place for you but...the archbishop will explain! We will go to the archbishop tomorrow morning."

"But what about tonight? Where are we to spend the night?"

"We will take you to a rooming house nearby!"

As they walked to the rooming house, the sisters stared at the garbage-lined streets and sidewalks. To make matters worse, a mouse scurried across their rented room and the bed sheets were filthy. But nothing could dim Mother Cabrini's optimism.

"Don't worry, my daughters.... For tonight let us rest as well as we can on these chairs! God is so good. He loves us and wants us to return that love by cheerfully offering these little sacrifices."

When the sisters were asleep, Mother Cabrini knelt on the hard, dirty floor and poured out her fears to the Sacred Heart. She prayed for hours. After Mass and Communion the following morning, the sisters went for their meeting with the spiritual leader of New York's Catholics, Archbishop Corrigan. The archbishop smiled warmly; then the smile faded and he asked: "Why are you here?... I wrote you stating not to come. We can't possibly start another orphanage now.... I want you to go back on the same ship that brought you!"

There was silence...but only for a moment, because a small nun stepped forward. Her transparent blue eyes pierced the stately archbishop to the core, as she said softly, "Your Excellency, we were sent here by the Pope. You see, we *cannot* go back! We have been entrusted with a special task and I will not rest until we fulfill it!"

Her answer stunned him. Archbishop Corrigan's face reddened as he demanded, "Let me see your credentials!"

She handed the papers to him. There was a tense silence and then, "Of course you will remain.... It is the Holy Father's wish."

Then the archbishop smiled and rubbed his chin. He glanced down at the radiant face of Mother Cabrini.

Mother Cabrini began her work among the Italian immigrants for whom she established orphanages, schools and adult classes in Christian doctrine. The spirit of self-sacrifice and joyful giving that filled her whole soul radiated about her like the bright warmth of a candle's glow. And the light continued to burn as she began one charitable work after another like Columbus Hospital in Manhattan. It happened like this:

Two of her sisters were visiting patients in a city hospital one day. A patient overheard them speaking his native Italian language and he called to them excitedly.

"Sisters, come to see me, too,...please pray with me."

"Of course we will.... What is your name? What part of Italy do you come from?"

The suffering face of the man shone with joy as he shared the sisters' company. Then, painfully, he opened the drawer of the night stand next to his bed and pulled out an unopened letter.

"Sisters,...I received this letter three months ago from my family back home.... But I don't know how to read. Will you read it to me?"

One of the sisters took the letter from his hand and glanced at the carefully penned message. Her voice trembled as she informed him of the reason for the note: "My friend,...your mother...has passed away!"

The man wept, and the sisters wept, too. When they went home and related the event to Mother Cabrini, it was her turn to weep. But her tears were soon action! With Archbishop Corrigan's permission, Mother Cabrini began her own hospital.

Soon enough patients filled the two adjacent houses that were the nucleus of Columbus Hospital. The sick and dying who came there weren't attracted by modern conveniences—there was no gas and no water. The rooms were bare...but the people wanted to stay anyway. News traveled up and down the streets of New York about the love and dedication that motivated Mother Cabrini and her sisters. And help began to pour in....

When the sisters were asleep, Mother Cabrini knelt on the hard, dirty floor and poured out her fears to the Sacred Heart. She prayed for hours.

"Sister, I'm a doctor.... I will donate my services free to any and all of your patients...."

"Sister, my boss said you can pay for the medical instruments whenever possible. There's no rush. You do wonderful work."

"Mother Cabrini, please accept my donation. It should cover the purchase of at least ten beds and sheets!"

There were also those who opposed the foundation of Columbus Hospital, but they were drowned out by the enthusiasm of the majority who helped. There was no doubt about it, the rays that glowed from Mother Cabrini inspired and ennobled those whom she met.

Sister Frances Xavier Cabrini became a United States citizen in 1909 and was elected Superior General of her religious community for life. She founded convent schools, orphanages, and hospitals throughout the United States, South America and Europe. She and her sisters visited the sick, men and women in prisons, the poor, the lonely, the suspect.

Mother Cabrini crossed the Atlantic Ocean thirty times and within thirty-five years she established sixty-seven convents. Yet these monumental deeds did not detract from the simplicity that enshrined her whole being.

Once as she walked across the school yard, a little girl pulled her hand free from her mother's grasp, and ran up to the famous nun.

"Hi, Sister.... I like you...you're nice!"

Mother Cabrini smiled, put her arm around the little stranger, and said, "I like you, too! And here's something just for you!"

She pressed a shining medal of the Sacred Heart into the child's hand.

"For me?...to keep forever?"

Mother Cabrini responded happily, "Yes on both counts—for *you* and...to keep forever!"

The child ran back to her mother displaying the shiny medal. The surprised mother watched with admiration as Mother Cabrini continued across the playground. The young mother said half to herself, half out loud: "Some people are like walking sunshine. They spread happiness wherever they go."

Mother Cabrini died in Chicago on December 22, 1917. Quick in life and in death, she was canonized just twenty-nine years later in 1946. If only one word could be chosen to adequately summarize Mother Cabrini, that word could well be *missionary*. St. Frances Xavier Cabrini's definition of a missionary is a resumé of her own incredible life...:

"What is a missionary? To me a missionary is an uncompromising lover of the Sacred Heart. She is *His candle* that radiates light while she consumes her life embracing everything—labors, joys and pains—for the salvation of all people.

22

the banker's daughter

The banker's daughter stood at the window, and playful sunlight daubed at the letter she held in her hand. Images and events tumbled through her memory in kaleidoscopic fashion: the gala trips to Europe, the society debuts and balls, the endless whirl of socializing, entertaining, being entertained.... So much, so *very* much had been happening. And so fast!

Kate Drexel again looked at the postmark: "Omaha, Nebraska." Just a few months ago the sight of it would have meant sheer joy. Now it meant sheer torture.

Of *course* she wanted to be a nun! Why, for years she had longed to get off the relentless merry-go-round that was high society in the elegant eighties. And finally

she had wrung the permission from Bishop O'Connor.
Now God, and God only, was to be her portion forever.
The convent she had yearned for was soon to be hers. She
couldn't wait for the day when she would be able to sign
away her wealth and at last be blissfully, totally poor....
The cloister appealed to her strongly. All that she wanted
was to be a nun, a simple, ordinary sister spending her
life in quiet prayer and service.... *That* wasn't bothering
her at all. But something else was.

Kate shook herself from her thoughts and forced
herself to re-scan the letter's close handwriting. She again
skimmed the beginning with all its prayerful greetings
and politeness and focused on that thunderbolt of a para-
graph:

"...The more I have thought of your case, the more
convinced I become that God has called you to *establish
an order* to help the Indian and Black people. The need
for it is clear to everybody.... You have the means to
make such an establishment. God has put in your heart a
great love for the Indian and the Negro. He has given you
a taste and a capacity for the sort of business which such a
foundation would bring with it. All these things point to
your duty more clearly than an inspiration or a revelation
could....

"I was never so sure of any vocation, not even of my
own, as I am about yours. If you do not establish the
order in question, you will allow to pass an opportunity
of doing immense service to the Church, which may not
occur again...."

"I can't! I just *can't!*" Kate's heart pounded. Everything in her recoiled from the idea of being a Foundress.
Found a order? What of her desire for prayer and solitude? And what about religious formation? Why, she
didn't have the faintest idea of how a postulant should
act, never mind establish an entirely new religious community! Besides, the whole thing might be one disastrous

failure; she might even do more harm than good.... The objections seemed to jostle one another into the foreground.

But there it was—the will of God—in Bishop O'Connor's own handwriting.

Really, it had been her own "fault." To say that Katherine Drexel had long considered full-time dedication to the American Indian and Black population her mission in life was an understatement. She had been giving continually of her wealth and had done all in her power to encourage others of means to do the same. Her family funds had already built missions and schools, obtained better housing and raised educational levels. When on a pilgrimage to Rome, she had presented further desires and plans to the Pope, begging him for missionaries for the Black and Indian apostolate. And with that piercing yet fatherly gaze of his, Leo XIII had leaned forward with a confidential, knowing smile.

"Why not become a missionary *yourself*, my child?" the Holy Father had asked.

And here was Bishop O'Connor's letter saying the same thing. Suddenly the whole weight of her approaching responsibilities pressed on Katherine's very being like a leaden yoke. Yet, this was what God wanted.

"Your will—not mine—be done," she murmured.

This was not to be the last time Katherine Drexel would say those words.

"Your will—not mine—be done."

Katherine—*Sister* Katherine now—pronounced the words slowly, for herself and her God. Her world seemed to be crumbling. Death had snatched away the one she had relied on, her trusted spiritual father and friend, Bishop O'Connor. He had "gone to God" as the saying went, but that wasn't much consolation to her. The young novice felt alone. Utterly alone. The bishop was gone. The work, the new community, the rule, the whole plan had been under his direction. She had counted on him, and the bitter feeling of her own uselessness and helplessness flooded Sister Katherine's soul. The temptation came strongly, and it would keep coming back: "Give up, give up. Forget the whole idea."

She could enter the community where she was making her novitiate—an older, secure order. She could settle down to a normal religious life, as she had wanted to do in the first place. She hungered for that security. The future seemed like one great, dark unknown.... Surely God would understand....

But the bishop's words rang clear, hauntingly clear:

"If you do not establish this order, you will allow to pass an opportunity of doing immense service to the Church, *which may never occur again....*"

This was God's doing, not hers. She had to go ahead.

On February 12, 1891, Katherine Drexel became the first Sister of the Blessed Sacrament for Indians and Colored People. To the three religious vows of chastity, poverty and obedience, she added a fourth—the dedication of her entire life to the service of the Indian and Black races of America.

Years passed. The young community grew and its work expanded. To the Southwest, the far West, the mid-South and the deep South, then east and north went Mother Drexel's spiritual daughters. Soon not only the sisters, but all those to whom she gave herself so generously knew that "Mother" was not merely a title for this remarkable woman. It was a way of life.

Indians of every tribe: Navajos, Pueblos, Papágos, the Osage, the Creek, Choctaw and Chickasawas..., Blacks across the country, from Philadelphia to bayou settlements, from Georgia to the industrial cities of the North—all felt the warmth of her love.

For Katherine Drexel, love was constructive. This woman of quiet dignity, whose former social life had introduced her to the whirlwind of city glamor, was starkly aware of one thing: what the elite of society, what tourists see is one thing. What missionaries and the people they serve see, is another.

When Mother Katherine sent her sisters to the great American cities, so rich in culture and traditions, she was keenly aware that the people who had created these masterpieces of cultural splendor were of varied backgrounds. She did not view America as a melting pot, but rather as a vivid mosaic, in which every color, every hue of tradition and race, brought out the beauty of the whole.

If fearfulness and hesitancy had marked the young socialite at the beginning of her work, a humble self-assurance and determination now characterized Mother Drexel, the Foundress, when it came to the accomplishment of her community's mission.

Again Katherine Drexel stood with letter in hand—a Katherine far more stately than the vivacious young woman who had cringed at Bishop O'Connor's request.

Years had matured her beautiful qualities—her gentleness, her compassion—and had deepened that marvelous practicality and keen business sense that the banker's daughter had inherited along with his millions. Time had also deepened the overpowering love she felt for Christ in the person of His Black and Indian brothers. It was this same love, fanned into flame, that year after year, day after day, had consumed itself to destroy hatred, bigotry, prejudice and misunderstanding.

This was the Katherine Drexel who scanned the letter.

She had purchased land in the South to establish a school for black children. The deed had been signed, the papers all processed. Now the former owner was insisting on retracting the deal. He had been ignorant, he wrote vehemently, of the purpose the land was to be used for. He would give the money back, with the commission he had made, but he insisted that the land be returned to him. That was the content of the letter.

Nor did it go along unanswered. In her simple dignity Mother Drexel replied. She explained, clarified points, soothed. With the sharp insight of a banker's daughter and true businesswoman, she spelled out particulars, and she refused to back down. With the Christlike spiritual leadership that was distinctively hers, she pointed out that more than property was in question when she said, "...And so, temporal things, after all, are only to be valued inasmuch as they bring us and many others—as many as possible—to the same eternal joys for which we were all created...."

When the furor continued to rage, Mother Drexel held her ground, in a combination characteristic of the great: with great kindness and humility, without rancor, and with the firm determination that this was, after all, God's cause, not hers. God would have to provide—and He did.

Katherine Drexel would have smiled at the prospect of being considered a leader in the cause of civil rights. Yet almost single-handedly, without billboards or bumper stickers, without rallies or editorials, she was waging a campaign for millions of emerging Americans. And noiselessly, steadily, she was winning. Decades before they were spoken, the banker's daughter made a life-program of the words of Pope Paul VI: "Peace must be *built:* it must be built up, every day, by works of peace."

She was working for the cause of Christian brotherhood. And brotherhood is peace.

A remarkable American, a remarkable woman, Katherine Drexel was equally remarkable as a religious. The vast chain of undertakings that involved the usual red tape of legalism, mounds of paperwork, statistics and financial reports without end—never for a moment were allowed to obscure her vision of her goal: the glory of God and the good of His people. She was not always understood; her work frequently met public disapproval, hostility. It didn't matter. As she wrote to her closest associates, "...They can think of me however they wish. All that we are here to accomplish is the mission that God has entrusted to us. We want to fulfill His will quietly, without fanfare. Remember, Sisters, do not seek to be praised, because only God sees the heart."

"We are here to do God's work."

For Katherine Drexel it was that simple.

As a sister, she never owned a penny herself, but her family fortune was tabulated in millions. The days she spent in travel turned into years, yet her heart's desire had been the silence of the cloister. Statesmen, leaders of all races, tribal chieftains, reporters, missionaries—all sought out the nun who had yearned to simply fade into the background.

During Jesus' public life, a rich young man "went away sad" because his great wealth meant more to him than Christ.

Nineteen centuries later, a rich young woman reversed all that. With the very rashness of a lover, she threw at Christ's feet not only all her wealth, but all her life as well, and took up the cry of the Master Himself:

"I came that they may have life
and have it to the full"!

Truly, America today is richer—because of a banker's daughter.

23

the
road
to
Mount
Royal

It was a cold November afternoon in 1897. Father Gastineau paced back and forth in his office at the Notre Dame School of Montreal, Canada. The sharp winds, which rattled the windows now and then, seemed to increase his nervousness. He halted a moment, turned around to face the young priest in front of him, and then began, "I know Brother Andre can't do much in the line of teaching, but he *is* a tremendous help in keeping this school in order. Not everyone in this world is called to be a teacher. Imagine what a mess we would be in if someone didn't answer the door, sweep the halls, mend our clothes and take care of the sick brothers. I'd like to see *you* scrub the floors of this ramshackle old building. You'd probably wind up with a bucket stuck on your head!"

"Yes, Father," the young priest replied, "but I still think Brother Andre belongs in a shoe factory instead of our college. All he'll ever accomplish in life is the embarrassment of our community."

"Now, now," the superior answered, "if you are *that* learned in theology, philosophy and all the sciences, I think it's about time you come down to earth and realize that there is more to life than the knowledge found in books. There is a greater knowledge which comes from God—it's called faith."

Brother Andre sat at his desk, trying to repair a shoe. From the tall, narrow window of the room, he looked out across a snow-covered field toward the steep side of Mount Royal.

More than fifty years of his life had slipped by. His once coal black hair had turned white. Pain and grief were written on his face. Time seemed to be running out. All the goals he wanted to reach seemed distant. Would he let his greatest dream be shattered? Or would he turn the slope of Mount Royal into a shrine in honor of Saint Joseph, patron saint of Canada?

Until now the students of the Notre Dame School had used the slope as their favorite picnic spot, and the brothers went there often to meditate.

He wondered how a shrine could be built on the property. What would people think? What would the brothers and his superiors say? Despite all these questions, he still envisioned a beginning, no matter how insignificant. After all, Christ started His Church with only a handful of poor, ignorant fishermen.

One day in the summer of 1904, Brother Andre worked his way up to the crest of Mount Royal. The day was cool, and as he reached the top, he could hear the busy drum of the city below.

Little did the people of Montreal know that God was working in their midst to lay the foundation of the world-famous Oratory of St. Joseph.

Brother Andre placed the statue of St. Joseph, which he had been carrying, in a cave near the top of the hill. He thought of the time in St. Joseph's life when the peo-

Brother Andre sat at his desk, trying to repair a shoe. From the tall, narrow window of the room, he looked out across a snow-covered field toward the steep side of Mount Royal.

ple in Bethlehem had not realized that the Son of God was being born in their town. St. Joseph had not demanded a palace for Mary and the Christ Child. Instead he sought out a humble dwelling.

Like St. Joseph, Brother Andre put everything in the hands of God. It wasn't long before the little brother was busy with several other brothers in working to build the first chapel of St. Joseph on Mount Royal. With the passing of time this chapel proved to be too small to hold the increasing number of pilgrims.

In answer to the new problem, Brother Andre thought of a plan.

One morning he asked his superior, "Father, here are five hundred dollars which the pilgrims have given me to enlarge the chapel. When should we begin the work?"

At first the superior did not understand the question. When he did, however, he looked at the brother and roared, "*What is this*, Brother Andre? You must be crazy! Do you want a *basilica* up there?"

Brother Andre paused and then nodded, "Yes." The superior frowned a moment and then shook his head. He didn't know what to say. It wasn't every day that one of the brothers handed him five hundred dollars with the request to build a chapel dedicated to St. Joseph. While he battled within himself to reach a conclusion, he decided that perhaps God was behind the plans of Brother Andre. He granted permission for the building of a new chapel. The next day Brother Andre set to work.

Soon after Brother Andre's sixty-fifth birthday, he received the duty of being the Official Guardian of the Chapel of St. Joseph. The Archbishop of Montreal began an investigation of the shrine. When he finished, he asked the superior, "If I ask Brother Andre to stop his work, will he obey me?"

"Why, yes, Your Excellency."

"Very well, then let him continue. If it is the will of God, the work will grow. If not, it will collapse. Let him continue!"

And with the grace of God, the work progressed.

One day Brother Andre heard the door of his office creak open. A reporter from the Montreal newspaper approached the brother seated at his desk.

After introducing himself, the visitor asked, "Brother Andre, how old are you? Many often wonder since you seem so young."

"*Old?*" the little brother questioned. "I'm not old. Seven and five makes twelve, which means I'm twelve years old."

"But don't you ever feel tired and worn out?"

"Tired?... Can anyone ever be tired in the service of the Lord?"

Another reporter spoke with Brother Andre, who was ninety-one at the time. The reporter wrote: "Brother Andre stood only about five feet tall. While I was in his office talking to him, he suddenly jumped up. He leaped on a chair and from there to a nearby radiator-top. Then he started to wind a grandfather's clock. You'd never believe that he had just celebrated his ninety-first birthday several days before...."

The end drew near. One of his old friends, Father Clement, went to visit him. After they exchanged greetings, Father Clement noticed the joy on the face of Brother Andre.

"Why are you so happy?" he asked.

"I was thinking that in a year or two Christmas Mass will be celebrated in the basilica."

"Well," Father Clement smiled, "certainly you'll be there for that glorious day."

"No, Father," the brother replied with a touch of sadness. "This is the last Christmas I will have on earth."

"But don't you realize we need your help?"

"My work is done, and anyway, if a person is able to do good here on earth, just imagine how much more he can do in heaven."

Towards the end of Brother Andre's last sickness, the superior decided to bring him to the hospital. The brothers carefully wrapped him up in many blankets so as to protect him from the bitter January cold. When they finished, all they could see of him was his face.

Wondering why he kept receiving puzzled looks, he grinned and remarked, "Well, I guess I look like somebody bound for the North Pole."

Everyone chuckled, but their laughter was short-lived. They knew their beloved Brother Andre would not be with them much longer.

After arriving at the hospital, his superior asked, "Are you suffering much?"

"Yes, I'm suffering, Father. But I thank God for giving me the grace of suffering because I greatly need it. We do not think enough about death."

The superior looked at the ninety-four-year-old brother who had always been the life of the community. Brother Andre never seemed to grow old. He had been active up to the last week of his life.

Not even the thought of death stopped him. It made him more fervent in the service of the Lord. He had always been busy, fiery and quick. For more than forty years he had worked among the sick in their homes and in hospitals. He had gone to cheer up the old people, to bring the light of Christ's message of peace to those in prison. When he hadn't been busy with answering the door or doing some task for the brothers, he went out to visit those who needed prayer and hope, laughter and comfort in the midst of their sufferings.

His life had been a full one—spent entirely for God. He often told others, "Heaven is so beautiful that it is worth all the trouble we put into our preparation for it." The thought of heaven was his guiding light, and his secret was this: to use every fiber of his being, every ounce of his strength, to earn the eternal reward of heaven not only for himself, but also for his companions in Christ.

Moments before he died, Brother Andre glanced at those who surrounded his bed. He took a deep breath and began: "You do not know all the blessings which the good God gave us at the Oratory. What misery there is in the world! I thank God for having given me the grace to relieve some of it. God is the One who helped me—just look at His power! How good He is, how beautiful! If our soul is only a glimpse of His beauty, He must be infinitely beautiful!"

Then he whispered, "O Mary, my good Mother, and Mother of our Savior, be kind to me and help me."

He stopped a moment and added softly, "Saint Joseph...."

A great silence followed.

Brother Andre, a simple doorkeeper of the Notre Dame School in Montreal, brought a love for St. Joseph into the hearts of thousands. He left behind him the example of one who had the faith to believe and the determination to reach his purpose in life.

24

**young
sheep
in
the
briars**

The meadow grass rustled and frantic bleating of sheep shook the calm afternoon. Six-year-old Eddie Flanagan heard the cries and broke into a run in search of the victim sheep. He stopped short of a boundary trench. There, trapped in the thorns, was a young lamb. Trembling with determination, Eddie began the rescue. His hands bled as, one by one, he gently picked out the briars, until the animal was free.

"It's all right! Everything's going to be all right. Come on, get up on my shoulders.... That's the way. Now, let's go home!"

Eddie never even imagined on that sunny day in Ireland that this incident would somehow become characteristic of his whole future life as a priest-shepherd laboring for Christ in far-off America.

Edward Joseph Flanagan completed his studies, and was ordained a priest on July 26, 1912. There was no time to lose. So many sheep were caught in the brambles, but the sheep were *people* who needed Christ and a priest to bring Christ to them.

And so it was to Omaha, Nebraska, that the young Father Flanagan went. The Omaha of *his* day was a stopover for migrant harvesters, and in that summer of 1913 the crops were very scarce. The work awaiting the priest was urgent and overwhelming. People were in need...the painful briars to be taken away were hunger, unemployment, loneliness and sin.

Father Flanagan walked into the grocery store mumbling. "There must be a way to help them. We can't let them starve."

The grocer overheard the remark and detected the worry. "You're right about that, Father. Being the grocer, I see their misery and sufferin'. What's to be done about these harvesters, eh? They sit there from morning till night waiting, just waiting. They'll start dying off one of these days right out in front of my store. It's a fact, man, no one can live without eatin'...."

"I know.... I know!"

And so, for the next hour, a discussion went on between the anxious priest and the concerned grocer. In the end a plan emerged. The priest agreed to pay for part of the needed food from his meager salary of $25.00 a month with the storekeeper matching him. Both would solicit additional help from friends. A systematic food rationing program was set up. But that wasn't enough. Father Flanagan asked himself, "How can I get into my warm bed at night...how can I sleep when I see men huddled on the ground or sleeping on coal piles and wooden planks?"

"Father in heaven, let me be Your means of bringing peace and comfort to Your suffering, jobless sons. I want to bring You to them. Show me the way."

And God did show the way. Father Flanagan's prayer was answered when he took over an old, rundown hotel. His dream of a free hotel for homeless men became a reality. Eventually, Father Flanagan's hotel housed the most unique guests. Yes, that's what he called them— guests. While their fellow men called them thieves, gangsters, drug addicts and murderers, to Father Flanagan they were "guests." Any man in need of food, shelter and understanding could count on him!

And then one night...a small boy, shivering and dirty, walked through the front door. Father Flanagan was sitting alone in the hotel lobby.

"Can I stay here?"

Father Flanagan knelt down beside him and asked softly, "Why do you want to stay here?"

"I heard you let people live here for nothin'," the boy replied.

"That's right, but not young boys like you. You must have your own house with your mommy and daddy."

"No, I ain't got nothin' like that."

Slowly the story fitted together like the pieces of a jagged crossword puzzle. His name was Jimmy. He was nine years old. His mother had died a few weeks before. He had never known a father. He hadn't had anything to eat for twenty-four hours and had been sleeping outside for a few nights. The priest patted the boy on the head and said more to himself than to the lad: "A lot of briars to remove from such a little fellow.... Best to begin right now...."

After some supper and a brisk bout with the wash cloth, Jimmy was tucked into bed. "Father, this bed sure is soft and warm.... Hey, Father, you know what? My mother sure was pretty. She was the best lookin' mother in the whole world. And you know what too, Father? You look an awful lot like her."

The priest smiled—that famous Flanagan smile—and then closed the door quietly. A long night of thinking and praying lay ahead. Father Flanagan covered his face with his hands. For more than three years he had been working with men who were in desperate need of remaking their lives, but except for a few, they hadn't responded. Some told him they didn't care, that it was too late for them. But...it wasn't too late for boys like Jimmy.

Perhaps the work had to begin when the clay was still pliable, when the man was still a boy. Father Flanagan set aside a few separate rooms of his hotel for young guests—for boys.

He also began to search out the juvenile courts. He was appalled because young delinquents were being tried as adult criminals. How often he was to utter these now famous words: "There's no such thing as a bad boy!"

Then one day, a murmur ran through the courtroom at the judge's return. "All right, Father Flanagan, I'm going to give you what you asked for. I'm paroling them in your charge. Good luck."

In silent astonishment, the seven little "gangsters" of Denton Street filed out onto the sidewalk, led by the amazing young priest. They were expecting a sermon but got a baseball game instead.

"Hey, here's a great spot for home base!"

"Yeah, and this rock can be second, and the pitcher's mound can...."

Above their yelling, Father Flanagan shouted, "You'll all keep on living at home, but we'll meet together here at the baseball field three nights a week after supper. Agreed?"

"Agreed," they chorused.

They *did* come back, every one of them! After each baseball game, the boys gathered around Father to talk things over...their problems, their needs. Soon more and more troubled boys were paroled into his care. Father Flanagan realized the need for a better way of meeting and caring for them. The park bench was becoming much too crowded! The time had come to begin the great undertaking that was to become *Boys Town!* Father Flanagan knew that it wasn't going to be easy. He had his share of problems and opposition, but he went ahead and began his home for boys which was destined to become so much to so many!

Some time later a box car conversation was going on in a train in far off Pennsylvania between an old man and a twelve-year-old boy.

"What are ya gawking at, boy?"

"Uh, oh...nothin'...."

"Ya look scared. Don't be. Come o'er here. What's ya name?"

"Tommy, and I'm runnin' away from home!"

"What for?"

"My dad died and Mom got married again."

"Yeah?"

"Now Mom died, too. That man she married don't want me around—says he doesn't care if I live or die...."

"Where ya' headin' for now, Tommy?"

"Anywhere."

"Listen, boy. I've got an idea. There's this priest I know..., used to run a hotel for guys like me, but he closed that down and opened up a new place for kids just like you. Imagine, a town just for boys—with hot food, and a warm bed, and a baseball diamond."

"Stop it. Stop it. You gotta be lyin'!"

"No, I'm given it to ya straight. It's for real! Yep, that's what they call it: BOYS TOWN!"

Tommy squinted hard to make out the letters engraved in the stone: B-O-Y-S T-O-W-N...BOYS TOWN!

Tommy had "begged" and "stolen" his way from Pennsylvania to Omaha, Nebraska, on the word of an old man in a railroad car. He met Father Flanagan. His face glowed with expectation as he voiced this simple request:

"Father, can I stay here? Can I live with you?"

"Sure, Tommy. You need us, and we could sure use another hand out at the dairy, so you're in. Here to stay! You've got a home again, Tommy!"

Tears blurred Tommy's eyes. When he wiped them away, he saw that Father was pointing to a little blue ceramic statue of a lady praying.

"That's Mary, you know, Jesus' Mother. Talk to her when you pray; she's always ready to be a mother to everyone. Good night now, Tommy."

This was how Father Flanagan's BOYS TOWN grew. The whole town was run by the boys—boys just like Tommy. They had their own government, their own post office, their own bank accounts, their own payrolls for chores they worked at in Boys Town. The old hobo had been right. Boys Town was everything he had told Tommy it was! There was even a trade school complex including everything from a bakery and machine shop to a barbershop and barnyard—all run by boys. And there was a chapel, too.

At age sixty-two, the man who with God's help had brought this wonderful town into existence, was growing a little tired, but that didn't temper his pace. At the request of the United States War Department, Father Flanagan left for wartorn Europe in 1948 to survey and report on youth conditions in Austria and Germany.

No one could ever guess that for Father Flanagan the good-byes and embraces of Boys Town were to be the last. In the early morning hours of May 15th, the shepherd's life came to an unassuming end in a distant Berlin hospital. He was gone...from this earth anyway. But people like Father Flanagan never really die because the love that lit his life continues to glow, whenever a person anywhere in this world reaches out—in Christ's name—to help his neighbor and to remove the briars of hunger, loneliness, and the haunting nightmare of being unloved.

Father Flanagan's love for boys will never be forgotten. For as someone once said: "A man never stands so tall as when he stoops to help a boy."

"A man never stands so tall as when he stoops to help a boy."

25

"victory
of
victories"

It was an important moment in the history of Father Baker's foundations. A crew of oil drillers looked on intently as the prayerful priest set a small statue of Our Lady of Victory on the ground. With uncommon serenity and a gentle self-assurance which could only come from familiarity with God, the priest faced the workers' uneasy glances.

"This is the spot. Put your drill down here, as close to the statue as you can—but without touching it," Father explained.

The drillers looked at the statue, and then at one another. They had come from the Pennsylvania oil fields to Limestone Hill near Buffalo, New York, to drill for natural gas. All calculations and reports were discouraging and pessimistic. No geologist or engineer had determined the spot. This Father Baker had simply chosen the end of his "prayer path" for the location! And yet, he seemed so sure of himself. His optimism was disarming and his sparkling expectation contagious. He must know something we don't know, the drillers thought to themselves. And with that, the drilling began.

It was not a phantasy or whim that had initiated the plan. Father Baker had prayed arduously and confidently, and had entrusted the entire project to Our Lady of Victory. This find of natural gas which he hoped for would supply the various charities he operated at Victory Hill so that the money usually expended for heat and lighting could be used for more charity. There were the orphans, the sick, the unwed mothers, the poor, as well as the abandoned babies to be cared for. "Our Lady of Victory will not let them down," he had told the bishop. "She *will* provide!"

A month of drilling followed. The scorching sun burned the faces and backs of the men who had been watching the drill as it pounded 600, 800, 900, and even 1,000 feet into the ground. None of the dirt or rock extracted was the kind that is usually found near so much as a *pocket* of gas. Their enthusiasm waned quickly. Grumbling and discouragement began to pervade the tower area. "Why couldn't this money be used for the orphans rather than for this dry hole!" the men complained.

Finally the foreman confronted Father Baker. During the past month he had seen Father Baker's boys—the hospital, the sisters, and the religious brothers. There was so much good to be done, and the men were rightfully concerned! He just *had* to say something to Father about what had come to be called "Father Baker's Folly."

"I appreciate your concern," Father Baker confided. "It is my responsibility to care for the children and poor ones Our Lady of Victory sends to Victory Hill. If the money is being wasted, it is I who will have to answer to

God for it. Like a good mother, however, I am sure she will care for her own. You'll see. Put faith in Our Lady of Victory and keep drilling!"

And Father Baker never wavered. In spite of the ridicule and humiliation of apparent failure he was as serene as ever. "When we've shown enough faith," he would say, "Our Lady of Victory will provide for us."

And sure enough—she did. Not only did they find gas, but when the stream of it burst through, the impact blew one of the drillers right off his feet! The gas shot out uncontrollably and there was a terrible explosion. Flames soared eighty feet into the air.

Five men and three small boys were burned as they got too near the flames. The newspapers splashed the news in bold headlines. There *had* been a tremendous find!... Father Baker was exalted as a great pioneer.... Speculators were clamoring to purchase the land.... But there were three small boys badly burned. Little Eddie was in serious condition and might die. His brother, too, was burned, along with Fritz Walker. What did Father Baker have to say about them?

Father Baker did not appear alarmed or overly distraught. He went to see Eddie's mother as soon as he could and to check on the boys.

"Father, I'm so worried! The newspaper reports are *terrible*, Father. I'm so frightened. They say...they say... that...Eddie is going to *die!* Oh, Father, how could Our Lady of Victory let this happen?"

"Now, now, it's all right. Eddie is *not* going to die. He's going to be just fine—just wait and see. So is Joe and Fritz Walker—they're all going to be *all right.* Don't worry. Our Lady of Victory is taking care of them all!"

Father Baker told the boys the same as he visited them. He blessed them and pinned a medal of Our Lady of Victory on each of them. "You're going to be all right," he assured.

And once again he was right. To the astonishment of doctors and reporters, their recovery was phenomenal. Eddie—whom they thought would not recover—was doing so, and rapidly! In a few weeks his face had almost completely healed, without a trace of scars! His legs were healing too and he was already walking. Our Lady of Victory had done it again! The find of gas was her victory. This tragedy-turned-glory was *her* victory! Once again Father Baker found himself humbly kneeling before his favorite statue. With his characteristic pat on the cheek, he thanked this good Mother again. Then he got up to leave; after all, her little ones were waiting.

Every work Father Baker would undertake would first be entrusted to Our Lady of Victory, and it seemed that his faith was always rewarded. By the 25th year of his priesthood he was caring for over 1,500 boys. They had come from all over the U.S. The majority had arrived alone—they were unwanted.

From Colorado, Arkansas, Virginia—they traveled with no more than a label buttoned to their little jackets: "To Father Baker, Victoria, West Seneca, New York." Some came as young as six years old, and not one was ever sent away. Father Baker, by means of personal letters (which he called the Association of Our Lady of Victory) had spread his concern all over the country. To save the faith of these little boys, he asked that they be sent to him. They came by the hundreds—and somehow there was always just enough of everything necessary to care for them. At times there were cots in the halls and not an inch of space unused. Then, Father Baker would gladly give up his room. Often, a Brother of the Holy Infancy confided, Father would go to his easy chair in the office to say the breviary and *there* sleep until morning. That is, unless there was a serious problem to solve. In that case he would spend most of the night talking to Our Lady of Victory, in the chapel.

Father Baker's heart was ever open to new ways of providing charity for those most unfortunate. At one time the local papers carried numerous reports that many bodies of infants had been found in different parts of the city. Apparently they had been abandoned by their mothers who very often were unmarried and could find no one to help them care for them. Father Baker was profoundly moved as he read a story of the draining of a canal which had exposed the bones of infants and small children who had been drowned throughout the years. His heart was torn...what could he do? They were God's own creation, brought into this world by His love, and to be loved. *Something* had to be done for these innocent ones!

From this holy torment followed an intimate colloquy with Our Lady of Victory. Soon after, Father Baker rented a couple of rooms in Buffalo to begin a home for the unwanted infants. As soon as word spread, not even the whole building was sufficient to house them! In a few years the Infant Home was erected on Victory Hill, so that he could accommodate all the little ones sent to him. The acceptance procedure was very simple. A small bassinet, fully equipped with blanket and pillows, was left in the hallway, just inside the door. If she wished, any distressed mother could quietly open the door and leave her baby in the bassinet. There were no questions asked and no forms to fill out. Soon enough the baby would make his presence known—and there were the Sisters of St. Joseph always ready to care for him.

Father Baker took a personal interest in all the charities at Victory Hill. Each day after his administrative work was completed, he would visit with the babies at the Infant Home, covering their little feet, or holding a bottle for them. After he had visited all the wards, he would bless the babies and nurses for the night. Then he would visit the patients at the hospital next to the Infant

Home. In addition, there was the Orphan Home for children from five to ten years of age, the Protectory for those from ten to fifteen, and the Working Boys Home for those over fifteen years of age. All were welcomed, all were cared for, under the protection of Our Lady of Victory.

At one time in Buffalo, many men with large families were homeless and unemployed because of a steel strike. When Father Baker heard of it he sent for them. After paying the rent for their lodgings, he furnished them with food. As often as they came to see him, he would give them as many loaves of bread as they needed and a silver dollar to each. It was observed that if you got in line a dozen times Father Baker would just as freely give you that silver dollar! To complaints about his generosity he would simply reply: "Any man who takes the money and the bread needs it, or he wouldn't be here." In the language of charity, it was as simple as that.

In 1921, Father Baker's greatest dream was finally underway. He had labored and prayed tirelessly for years. He was now eighty-one years old. And it seemed that the hour had struck. He would announce his plans. There was to be a shrine to Our Lady of Victory—"with nothing in the world to compare to it." As usual there wasn't a nickel to start with, but Our Lady of Victory, yes, Our Lady of Victory would provide!

The magnificent shrine was elevated to the dignity of a basilica by Pope Benedict XV. It was the first basilica in the United States. It was dedicated in 1926, the year of Father Baker's Golden Jubilee of Ordination.

The basilica is a monument to charity and unbounded beneficence. It is a monument to the dedication of Father Baker and his faith in Our Lady of Victory. It is the center from which radiates a vast enterprise—hospitals, orphanages, maternity houses, asylums, workshops and schools—as well as a generous hand to all in any kind of need. Father Baker from this time on would spend much of his time kneeling in the basilica before the Blessed Sacrament. He was often observed talking to Our Lady of Victory. In his pocket there was an ever-ready supply of medals in her honor, freely dispensed to anyone who wanted one. Many miracles have been reported in the basilica—even while Father Baker was still alive.

Today the basilica stands—more vibrant than a memory—more magnificent than any monument. It is a powerful echo of the good done by one man—one man, that is, with the powerful help of that most loving Mother whom he called Our Lady of Victory. It was the crowning joy of a lifetime of work which had yielded two missions with a school and church; St. Joseph's Orphan Asylum, caring for about 200 boys during the year; Our Lady of Victory Infant Home, which by 1935 had cared for 6,500 infants and small children; Our Lady of Victory Hospital which cared for more than 3,000 sick people in one year, many of whom couldn't pay anything; Saint John's Protectory for hundreds of unwanted or wayward boys. At the time of Father Baker's death in 1936, over twenty-five thousand boys had been given shelter and work under his direction. These and all the personal acts of charity recorded only in heaven are some of the fruits of a life of prayer and faith, a life well lived, a life which could be called a victory of victories!

26

her
science
was
the
cross

Breslau, Germany, August, 1933. A train pulled into the station and a small woman in her early forties stepped out onto the platform. Fraulein Edith Stein greeted her sister, Rosa, who was waiting for her. The two women gathered up Edith's few suitcases and started for home.

Rosa struggled to hold her tongue in check. It seemed strange that her sister wasn't saying a word about her new tutoring position—if such it was. Edith had only sent a few vague lines about finding a place with some nuns at Cologne.... What a pity, Rosa thought again, that her sister—such a brilliant philosopher—had been forced by the Nazi government to turn to private teaching!

After a few silent moments, Rosa ventured, "Edith, why are you going to Cologne?"

Edith looked intently at her sister and knew she could confide her most guarded secret. "I've been accepted into the Carmelite convent there. But, I beg you, don't breathe a word of it to Mama. I must tell her myself."

"I promise, Edith," Rosa answered softly. "It's going to be very hard on Mama, very hard...."

"I know, Rosa. If my conversion caused her so much pain, I dread what will happen when I tell her what I'm going to do now."

Despite the sword that had severed the hearts of both mother and daughter in the past, old Frau Augusta Stein brightened up when Edith arrived home. This daughter, her seventh and youngest child, had long been her favorite, and it was good to have her home for these few weeks.

At first, everything went well. Though Frau Stein was in her eighty-fifth year, she went daily to her office in the lumber yard. She had built up the business herself after having been left a widow when Edith was only two. There was little business right now, however, due to the grave political situation. All that Frau Stein had worked and struggled for in her long life was falling around her in shambles. But the valiant matron would not allow herself to "rust out."

During the first weeks of Edith's visit, Frau Stein unburdened herself to her youngest daughter. Edith's calm attention and ready sympathy soothed the sorely-tried old woman. In the evenings, after returning from the office, Augusta would sit contentedly next to Edith and pour out her troubles of the present and the memories of the past while her still nimble fingers worked away at knitting. As the weeks seemingly dragged by, Edith dreaded the day that she would again have to break her mother's heart. The fateful hour came on the first Sunday of September.

Mama Stein sat down in her venerable armchair, pulled out her yarn and needles and began knitting. Without raising her eyes she asked, "Edith, what are you going to do with the Sisters at Cologne?"

"Live with them," Edith replied.

Immediately Frau Stein resisted with a desperate outburst. Her hands began to tremble violently. And, while mother and daughter clung to their own sides of the issue, Edith bent over to untangle the yarn.

"You're going to cut yourself off from me!" Frau Stein cried pathetically. "You're unfaithful! You, my most beloved daughter! Don't my tears count for anything? How can you just brush my grief aside? Where is your compassion for your old mother? Why must you do this? Why? Why?"

And so it went. When Augusta had exhausted herself in the outbursts of the first few days, she fell into periods of despair and silence.

Edith was later to write: "I knew my mother had become more silent because she secretly hoped I would not do what she thought was the most dreadful thing imaginable. I often wondered which one of us would break first, my mother or I. But we both held out to the last. Mama was inconsolable and I had to take the step in the utter darkness of faith." Edith was offering her life to God for the sake of her beloved Jewish people, and her love was interpreted as an act of desertion in their most needed hour.

Finally, October 12th arrived. It was Edith's birthday and her last day at home. Early that morning, mother and daughter were again pleading desperately with one another to understand and give in. But it was useless. That night the poor old woman buried her head in her hands and wept. Edith stood behind her chair and pressed her mother's silver head against her heart. They remained like that for a long time. At last, Edith took Frau Stein by the arm and led her up the stairs. For the first time in their lives, Edith helped her mother undress. Then she sat on the edge of the bed until the exhausted woman urged Edith to go to get some sleep. After a sleepless night and tearful embraces, Edith boarded the train that would take her to Cologne.

During the past weeks she had been immersed in a sea of futile discussions. Her mother's despair, her relatives' opposition, and the growing political dangers had thrown her into a whirlpool of doubt and confusion. So much so, that she sometimes had wondered if she were doing right or wrong in taking this step.

As the train pulled out of the station and the waving figures on the platform dissolved in the distance, Edith sank into her seat. There "was no rapturous joy"; the anguish of the last week had been too dreadful. But she "was perfectly at peace in the harbor of the divine will."

On October 14, 1933, forty-two-year-old Doctor Edith Stein, brilliant lecturer and philosopher, ceased to exist. And Postulant Edith Stein, of the cloistered Carmelites, began a new life. She was liked by all the sisters. Friendly and anxious to do her best, she took part in all the community duties and work. The Abbot of Euron wrote of her during this period: "At Carmel she was the only intellectual and she soon became the least of the sisters there."

She even had to learn how to hold and use a broom from a sister who was twenty years younger.

During her postulancy, Edith never dreamt of asking permission to continue her philosophical work, nor did she allow any of her friends to influence the abbess into giving permission to do so. But after having spent all her life in intellectual pursuits, Edith naturally found it very hard to adapt herself to manual tasks—including the arts of cleaning, cooking and sewing. She was clumsy and slow—even to an exasperating degree. But this was all part of her offering.

After two months, the former scholar admitted to her prioress, as she pointed to her head, "This machine here found it very difficult to learn all those little rules."

The prioress later wrote about Edith, "It almost seemed as if she had forgotten her past, all her knowledge and abilities, and had only the one desire of being a child among children."*

---

*The Scholar and the Cross, by Hilda C. Graef, Newman Press (Westminster, Maryland), 1956, p. 117.

On April 15, 1934, Edith Stein received her sacred habit and took the name Sister Teresa Benedict of the Cross. The provincial told her to continue her philosophical work and to begin writing right away. She would use her pen to make the Lord better known.

First vows, on April 21, 1935, were followed by final vows three years later.

At the same time the storm clouds of war were quickly gathering, and in this Sister Teresa Benedict had a constant reminder of the purpose of her offering—she would be a victim of expiation for the world and for her people, upon whom the cross of Christ had fallen.

Deep in the night of December 31, 1938, Edith Stein left her beloved community at Cologne to find refuge in the Carmel of Echt, Holland. Here in her new home with her new sisters, Sister Benedict quickly adapted herself and showed remarkable cheerfulness. She set to work immediately and took on new responsibilities. Among these was the writing of her studies of St. John of the Cross, which would later be published under the title, "The Science of the Cross."

In the spring of 1939, Sister Teresa Benedict asked her superior for permission to offer herself to the Sacred Heart of Jesus in a formal way as a sacrifice of atonement for the peace of the world. "Jesus deserves this sacrifice and He will doubtlessly request it of many other souls."

In the summer of 1940, Edith was joined by her sister, Rosa.

The persecutions were getting worse and someone suggested that Edith and Rosa escape. But Sister Benedict would not hear of it. Why, such an action would bring serious consequences on her whole community! No, she would leave her hand in that of God's loving Providence.

However, efforts were begun to obtain passports to Switzerland.

On August 2, 1942, as the sisters gathered in chapel for evening prayers, the front doorbell rang impatiently. Mother Prioress went to the parlor to find herself facing two policemen, who asked to see Sister Stein immediately. Thinking they brought news of the passports to Switzerland, the prioress called Sister Teresa Benedict, and she herself withdrew to the next room.

"Sister Stein," one guard ordered, "you are to leave here in five minutes!"

"I can't do that," Edith answered calmly. "We have strict enclosure."

"Remove that grille and come out!" shouted the officer.

"You'd better show me how to do that," quipped Edith.

"Call the superior immediately!"

The prioress was called and Sister Benedict went to kneel before the Blessed Sacrament.

"Sister Stein must come with us," the SS demanded.

"But she can't. Besides, she's waiting for her passport to Switzerland."

"That can be taken care of later," retorted the guard. "Tell her and her sister to pack and bring food sufficient for three days."

Five minutes later, Sister Benedict reappeared in the parlor, surrounded by her community. Sister Rosa knelt at the feet of the prioress to obtain her last blessing.

The Stein sisters were taken to a prison camp. An eyewitness described Edith: "Among the prisoners who arrived, Sister Benedict made a strong impression on me by her calmness and composure. Everyone was crying or confused and excited. The misery of the camp was appalling. Sister Benedict walked among the women and children, soothing and helping like an angel. Many mothers, who were almost mad with melancholy, brooding and hysterical weeping had neglected their children. Sister Benedict cared for the poor little ones, combed them, washed them and saw to it that they were fed and given attention. Everyone was amazed."

Another eyewitness commented on Edith's serenity: "My personal impression is that she suffered deeply but without anxiety. She would look with indescribable sadness at her sister Rosa: She was thinking, not of her own sufferings, but of everyone else's. She continually prayed and filled her soul with peace."

On August 7th, as a train carrying the prisoners wound its way eastward, a former student saw Edith standing in front of one of the windows, a picture of complete peace and serenity.

On August 9, 1942, Edith Stein—Sister Benedict—was executed. Her self-offering was now total; she had nothing more to give to God or her people.

27

the conquest

Dashing across the tennis court, sixteen-year-old Teresita Quevedo bumped into a girl she knew.

"Hi, Teresita," her friend called. "I hear you're signed up to win the tennis crown. Better warn them to get a large one; a normal size won't fit your head anymore."

Teresita laughed as she sped on in pursuit of the ball.

The evening after the final tournament, Mrs. Quevedo and her daughter met at home. Teresita greeted her mother with a smile.

"Well, Teresita," Mrs. Quevedo asked. "Are you going to tell me that we have a champion in the family?"

The girl paused a moment. Tears welled up in her eyes, but she tried to control them.

"No, Mama," she replied. "Not the kind you have in mind. But if you think of the winner of a spiritual victory as a champion, then you have a champion."

Mrs. Quevedo sat down on a couch, and motioned the girl to sit beside her. Perceptive, as all mothers are, the doctor's wife had long been aware of her daughter's desire to become a tennis champion before graduating from high school. Teresita had practiced for four years and had become a top-notch player.

Everyone had considered her to be the girl most likely to win because she had sailed effortlessly through all the other matches. But clearly God had willed otherwise.

"Mama," Teresita began, "this evening I stopped at church to tell the Blessed Mother I was happy she decided that my opponent should win the tennis crown instead of me. There was an old lady begging at the church door, and I gave her an offering. She motioned for me to wait, and then she gave me something. It was a holy card.... I noticed that there was no picture on the card, but rather an inscription in large blue print. Can you guess what it said, Mama?"

"No, Teresita—you tell me," Mrs. Quevedo replied.

With a determined air of victory, Teresita answered, "Love makes all things easy."

Some months later, one early afternoon, Teresita pried open the door to the room where her father was taking his siesta.

"Papa," she whispered, "are you asleep?"

"No, come in, Teresita," Doctor Quevedo invited. "Do you want something?"

"Yes, Papa, but if you want to sleep, I'll come back at another time."

"No, come in, dear," he answered.

Teresita walked over to her father's bed and stammered, "Papa, I dread telling you this, because it's going to hurt you, but...."

"Go on, tell me, Teresita. What is it you want?"

"I want to become a Carmelite, Papa."

"Teresita, do you realize what that means? You have always been so full of life—so fond of sports...dancing... and parties...." His voice trailed off.

"Yes, but none of that satisfies me, Papa."

"My dear child, do you know that to become a religious means to lead a life of sacrifice?"

"Yes, Papa, I know it. That is why I want to enter the convent."

"And," her father continued, "when do you want to enter?"

"Well, Papa, I've been thinking about that, too. I'd like to enter next month."

At first, Teresita's vocation was a bitter blow for Doctor Quevedo and his wife. How could they get along without their youngest daughter, who was so full of energy and enthusiasm? It would cost a great deal of sacrifice on their part to allow Teresita to enter the convent at the age of only seventeen.

But then, God's grace conquered their hearts, and Teresita's parents understood that her vocation was a blessing from God.

On February 23, 1947, Teresita Quevedo entered the Institute of the Carmelite Sisters of Charity, which was located in a little town just outside of Madrid.

Days turned into weeks and the weeks into months at the novitiate. Before Teresita knew it, profession was not far away. But neither was death.

One day, the young novice was walking down the hall to a classroom. Suddenly she winced from the pain throbbing in her head. Oh, well, she thought, maybe it's just another headache like the one I had yesterday. However, the pain increased, and Teresita could no longer concentrate on her work.

She went to talk to the superior, to tell her that she was suffering from a very severe headache. The superior sent Teresita to the infirmary to take some medication to relieve the pain. Two days later, she telephoned Doctor Quevedo and asked him to come to the novitiate.

He arrived within an hour and gave Teresita a thorough examination, only to discover that his daughter had tubercular meningitis.

With anguish tearing at his heart, Doctor Quevedo told the Reverend Mother, "My daughter will die in a matter of months. The best of care will not prevent it. Her case is not one of lifetime paralysis. A period of agony which is not far off will lead to her death."

One morning after Teresita had pronounced her vows, the sister in charge of the infirmary walked over to her bedside and asked, "Sister, don't you feel a bit sad when you think of leaving everything you love?"

"Why should I, Sister?" Teresita replied. "I'm not really leaving everything I love. I have a Father in heaven who is waiting for me and a Mother who will come to bring me to God. I've always loved our Lady; that is my greatest comfort now. Sister, if you loved our Lady with every fiber of your being—you would never suffer sadness, not even while looking death straight in the face."

Smiling down into Teresita's glowing eyes, the other sister felt impelled to say, "Everyone here knows that you have an extraordinary love of our Lady. How did you acquire it?"

"Only by trying to do the little things in life perfectly. True, there have been many difficulties I have had to overcome, and I have never done anything great in life. But I've found that Mary is a great means for reaching heaven. What I have done, I have done for God through Mary. My gifts to Mary have been little ones. But, I suppose, it's the little things in life that count."

"Little things done to perfection...it's the little things that count...." As the sister-nurse resumed her infirmary duties, she thought over Teresita's words. She thought, too, of little incidents that had taken place a few months earlier, before Teresita had become ill. Was it just a coincidence that especially on Saturdays and feasts of the Blessed Mother the sisters would be surprised to find their shoes "mysteriously" shined, or their stockings suddenly mended? Though nobody said anything, and Teresita never gave herself away, all the sisters knew she was "the culprit." The young sister had gone quietly from room to room, leaving behind shoes polished to perfection. Then she had slipped unnoticed into the laundry room and had rummaged through the mound of black stockings to darn a few pairs before the wash would be divided.

The infirmarian recalled another episode.

One of Teresita's fellow-novices had been bedridden in the infirmary. Worn-out by a long illness, she wasn't—naturally speaking—much company. She didn't feel like talking; she didn't want to read; she didn't even care to have the other sisters read to her. Whoever was to stay with her just had to resign herself to silence. Still, the superior wanted someone to spend at least the recreation period with the patient. She hoped for volunteers, but none was forthcoming—none except Teresita. Right before the eagerly-awaited recreation, she would ask, "Mother, could I spend recreation with Sister X today?" The request always ended with *today*, but the sister-nurse and the superior had noticed that "today" became day after day, for quite a while.... The permission was always granted. And Teresita, delighted at her triumph, would hurry off to the drab infirmary to spend an hour with the taciturn sister.

That must have been quite a sacrifice for her, mused the sister-nurse. For Teresita, so naturally joyful and exuberant, had looked forward to recreation more than all the other novices combined! She loved to chat and laugh, to enjoy the warm companionship and homey fun that bubbled up spontaneously among her sisters. Yet Teresita had sought out her quiet, suffering companion instead.

Her love for Mary played no small part in that victory. In her private notebook, Teresita had written, "May all who look at *me*, see *you*, O Mary!" And whether others knew of her resolution or not, it certainly wasn't hard to see the likeness of Mary mirrored in the joyful kindness of the young sister.

Death drew near Teresita gradually, until on Holy Saturday morning, April 8, 1950, it was only a few hours away. Pain racked every bone in her body, yet the young sister remained joyful and serene.

When her father, Doctor Quevedo, came to visit her that morning he realized that Teresita was on the verge of death. He thought back to when his younger daughter had been a little girl. He could still hear her screams of laughter and delight as she ran along the Spanish seacoast, chasing waves.

Then, as Doctor Quevedo sat helpless beside his dying daughter, watching her facial expression mirror the agony of her body, he thought back to an incident that had taken place a few summers before.

He had been at a swimming club one day when a lifeguard came up to say, "Doctor Quevedo, your daughter is an outstanding swimmer and diver. Has she ever entered a diving contest?"

"Juan," the doctor replied, "if you have in mind what I suspect you do, I don't encourage you to ask Teresita about it. She already declined one of my friends last summer when he asked her to join in the diving contests."

Juan thanked Doctor Quevedo and then went down to the beach to see if he could find Teresita. Well, he thought, Teresita *is* human. I'm sure that *I* can convince her to sign up. Never yet met a girl who refused me. I just don't understand how a girl like Teresita could say no in spite of all the trophies she would easily win.

Teresita had written, "May all who look at *me*, see *you*, O Mary!" And whether others knew of her resolution or not, it certainly wasn't hard to see the likeness of Mary mirrored in the joyful kindness of the young sister.

Minutes later he ran into Teresita. "May I speak with you for a minute?" he inquired. "I won't take much of your time, Miss Quevedo. I know you might be in a hurry...."

"No, Juan," Teresita replied. "I'm not in a hurry. Do you want something?"

"Well, Teresita, after speaking with your father not too long ago, I understand that you are an excellent swimmer. Why don't you take part in the diving contests which are coming up soon? None of the participants in your age bracket can match your speed or technique as a diver. Think of the honor it will give you and of the glory it will bring your parents!"

Teresita thought a moment before she answered. Then she said, "Juan, will it bring honor and glory to the Mother of God?"

For a second Juan was speechless. Teresita's decision hung upon the answer he was now searching for.

"Well, Teresita, let's leave her—I mean the Blessed Mother—out of this."

"OK, Juan, if that's what you really want...but I'll stay with our Lady."

Doctor Quevedo brought his thoughts back to the room where Teresita lay dying of a disease that medicine could not cure. As he looked at her, he felt so helpless and alone.

It took all the courage he had to just stand there and watch Teresita draw nearer and nearer to death. But thinking over her past life, he knew that there was one thing left to do: he could pray to the Blessed Mother for the strength he needed to accept God's will in his daughter's regard.

When the doctor received a telephone call the next morning, he answered in a natural tone of voice. The superior asked him to come as soon as possible. Teresita had passed to eternity.

When Doctor and Mrs. Quevedo reached the convent, the superior related the details. An aura of joy filled the air as she spoke....

Teresita had been sinking rapidly. The white bed that had become an altar trembled from the pain that racked her body, and she gave no sign of consciousness. Suddenly, she opened her eyes, and her usually-soft voice filled the room:

"My Mother, Mary, come for me! Bring me back to heaven with you!"

The community was summoned and filed prayerfully into the room. Strange, it seemed more like a cathedral than a death-chamber. The sisters knelt around Teresita's bed. She was quiet now, almost motionless except for the gentle rise and fall of the sheets with her labored breathing.

Then it happened, like the key note in a bursting crescendo, like a hymn of victory. The dying nun opened her eyes and a radiant smile lit her face for the last time: "Oh, how *beautiful!* O *Mary, how beautiful* you are!"

"Mary was her life," all those who knew Teresita had said. And Mary had come to lead her into the dawn of life eternal.

"O death, where is your victory? O death, where is your sting?... For death is swallowed up—in victory."

Teresita Quevedo had won. It was, indeed, *the conquest.*

Daughters of St. Paul

IN MASSACHUSETTS
   50 St. Paul's Ave. Jamaica Plain, Boston, MA 02130;
      617-522-8911; 617-522-0875;
   172 Tremont Street, Boston, MA 02111; 617-426-5464;
      617-426-4230
IN NEW YORK
   78 Fort Place, Staten Island, NY 10301; 212-447-5071
   59 East 43rd Street, New York, NY 10017; 212-986-7580
   7 State Street, New York, NY 10004; 212-447-5071
   625 East 187th Street, Bronx, NY 10458; 212-584-0440
   525 Main Street, Buffalo, NY 14203; 716-847-6044
IN NEW JERSEY
   Hudson Mall — Route 440 and Communipaw Ave.,
      Jersey City, NJ 07304; 201-433-7740
IN CONNECTICUT
   202 Fairfield Ave., Bridgeport, CT 06604; 203-335-9913
IN OHIO
   2105 Ontario St. (at Prospect Ave.), Cleveland, OH 44115; 216-621-9427
   25 E. Eighth Street, Cincinnati, OH 45202; 513-721-4838
IN PENNSYLVANIA
   1719 Chestnut Street, Philadelphia, PA 19103; 215-568-2638
IN FLORIDA
   2700 Biscayne Blvd., Miami, FL 33137; 305-573-1618
IN LOUISIANA
   4403 Veterans Memorial Blvd., Metairie, LA 70002; 504-887-7631;
      504-887-0113
   1800 South Acadian Thruway, P.O. Box 2028, Baton Rouge, LA 70821
      504-343-4057; 504-343-3814
IN MISSOURI
   1001 Pine Street (at North 10th), St. Louis, MO 63101; 314-621-0346;
      314-231-1034
IN ILLINOIS
   172 North Michigan Ave., Chicago, IL 60601; 312-346-4228;
      312-346-3240
IN TEXAS
   114 Main Plaza, San Antonio, TX 78205; 512-224-8101
IN CALIFORNIA
   1570 Fifth Avenue, San Diego, CA 92101; 714-232-1442
   46 Geary Street, San Francisco, CA 94108; 415-781-5180
IN HAWAII
   1143 Bishop Street, Honolulu, HI 96813; 808-521-2731
IN ALASKA
   750 West 5th Avenue, Anchorage AK 99501; 907-272-8183
IN CANADA
   3022 Dufferin Street, Toronto 395, Ontario, Canada
IN ENGLAND
   128, Notting Hill Gate, London W11 3QG, England
   133 Corporation Street, Birmingham B4 6PH, England
   5A-7 Royal Exchange Square, Glasgow G1 3AH, England
   82 Bold Street, Liverpool L1 4HR, England
IN AUSTRALIA
   58 Abbotsford Rd., Homebush, N.S.W., Sydney 2140, Australia